NEURO-DRIVEN MARKETING

UNLOCKING THE POWER OF SENSORY MEMORY TO CREATE IMPACTFUL BRANDS

MAHESH AGARWAL

STARDOM BOOKS

www.StardomBooks.com

STARDOM BOOKS
112 Bordeaux Ct.
Coppell, TX 75019, USA

Copyright © 2025 by Mahesh Agarwal

All rights reserved. No part of this book may be reproduced or used in any manner without written permission of the copyright owner except for the use of quotations in a book review.

FIRST EDITION AUGUST 2025

STARDOM BOOKS, LLC.
112 Bordeaux Ct. Coppell, TX 75019, USA

www.stardombooks.com

Stardom Books, United States
Stardom Alliance, India

The author and publishers have made all reasonable efforts to contact copyright holders for permission and apologize for any omissions or errors in the form of credits given. Corrections may be made to future editions.

NEURO-DRIVEN MARKETING
UNLOCKING THE POWER OF SENSORY MEMORY TO CREATE IMPACTFUL BRANDS

Mahesh Agarwal

p.237
cm. 13.5 X 21.5

Category: BUS043000 - Business & Economics : Marketing-General
BUS043060 - Business & Economics : Marketing-Research

ISBN: 978-1-957456-80-5

DEDICATION

To all bold marketers chasing fresh ideas to grow their brand

ACKNOWLEDGMENTS

Writing this book has been a long and rewarding journey — almost two years in the making — and I truly owe my deepest thanks to the people who made it possible.

First, a huge thank you to my dear friend Rajiv Lamba. It was his crazy, brilliant idea to start a neuroscience-based marketing research agency, and I'm so glad he brought me on this wild ride as a co-founder.

Big shoutout to my amazing team at Neurosensum — especially Arvind and Raj — for all the passion, sweat, and sleepless nights that went into building the neuro-products we're so proud of today.

To my kids, Kashika and Abhishek — thank you for all the curious questions, the honest reactions, and for helping me see things through a younger lens. Those little chats meant more than you know.

And finally — the biggest thanks of all — to my incredible wife, Kanchana. Thank you for your endless patience, your love, and for letting me disappear into my research bubble every weekend without ever complaining. Honestly, this book wouldn't exist without you.

CONTENTS

Introduction: Cracking the Code of the Consumer Brain   i

PART 1: Why Neuromarketing?

1. The Ancient, Energy-Hungry Human Brain   1
2. Moments of Truth and Brand Memory   13

PART 2: The Magic of Sound

3. Decoding Sonic Memory   23
4. Sonic Branding – The Music of Your Brand   27
5. Developing a Sonic Identity   35

PART 3: Visual Influence

6. Why Vision Is the Brain's Favorite Sense   41
7. How the Brain Stores What We See – Visual Memory   43
8. Visual Elements That Stick   51

PART 4: The Power of Touch

9. How Haptic Memory Works   59
10. Neuromarketing Applications of Touch   63

PART 5: Smell & Taste Synergy

11. How Smell & Taste Works   69
12. Leveraging Olfactory & Gustatory Memory in Marketing   73

PART 6: Experience Memory

13. When all your memories come together   79
14. How Experience Memory Shapes the 6Ps of Marketing   85

PART 7: The 6Ps and the Brain

15.	6Ps of Marketing from a Neuroscience Perspective	89
16.	Product Usage Memory	93
17.	Packaging Memory	99
18.	Pricing Memory	105
19.	Promotion Memory	111
20.	People Memory	117
21.	Process Memory	123

PART 8: Marketing Research Reinvented using Neuroscience

22.	Why Traditional Research Methods are not enough	131
23.	EEG (Electroencephalogram)	137
24.	Eye Tracking	143
25.	Facial Coding	149
26.	Implicit Association Testing (IAT)	155

PART 9: How "NeuroSensum" is helping Marketers

27.	The Evolution of Neuroscience and AI-based Marketing Research	163
28.	Neuroscience and AI-Based Marketing Research to Improve the 6Ps	167
	A: Neurosensum Myndsight	171
	B: Neurosensum MyndSensory	175
	C: Neurosensum MyndTune	179
	D: Neurosensum PackSense	183
	E: Neurosensum ShopperSense	187
	F: Neurosensum NeuroEquity Funnel	191

	G: Neurosensum NeuroImage	195
	H: SurveySensum Text Analytics (AI)	199

PART 10: Sensory Brand Audit

29.	Understanding & Using Your Brand Sensory Memory	205
30.	Putting Theory into Practice: Sensory Memory in Action	209
	References	217
	About the Author	219

INTRODUCTION

Cracking the Code of the Consumer Brain

Let's begin with a question every marketer has quietly asked themselves at some point: Why do some campaigns with perfect strategy, crisp visuals, and bulletproof logic still fail to move the needle?

I remember vividly a boardroom in Jakarta, 2016. We had just presented a campaign I believed was airtight. It had data-backed insights, precise segment targeting, stunning visuals, and a compelling narrative. Yet, when the campaign was launched, it flopped. Sales stagnated, and brand metrics barely moved. It was a punch to the gut.

That was my wake-up call.

What if the problem wasn't with the campaign but with how we were trying to reach the human brain? What if we were only speaking to the conscious mind while most decisions were happening in the shadows of the subconscious?

As I dug deeper, I stumbled upon a profound truth: Over 90% of our decisions are made subconsciously. Yes, nine out of ten choices you make today are quietly steered by instincts, emotions, and memory patterns your conscious self isn't even aware of. The human brain, after all, is an ancient machine built for survival.

It's always scanning, filtering, simplifying—taking shortcuts to preserve energy. And this is not laziness; it's evolutionary genius.

Our ancestors didn't have time to overthink whether a rustle in the bushes was wind or a predator. Their brains had to act fast.

Fast forward to today, and that same brain is choosing between cereal boxes, deciding whether to skip an ad, or feeling an unexplained trust for one brand over another. Welcome to the world of neuromarketing, where instinct meets insight.

Traditional marketing often stops at what people say. But what about what they feel? What their pupils dilate at? What their brain waves spike for? That's where neuroscience tools—like EEG, eye tracking, and facial coding—come into play. They help us go beyond the spoken word and into the unspoken truth.

Let me share a quick story. We once tested two ad creatives. The first was crowd-approved, safe, and liked in focus groups. The second was bolder and more emotional. EEG scans showed that the second ad activated the brain's reward and memory zones far more. When launched, it led to 27% higher recall and 19% higher impact.

The "riskier" ad, it turned out, was the one the brain remembered. That changed everything for me — and for the brands we worked with.

This book is born from that shift. It's not an academic journal nor a typical marketing manual. It's a storyteller's guide to the subconscious mind. You'll find:

Real stories from brands and campaigns

Complex neuroscience simplified and made usable

Frameworks that connect brain science with daily marketing

Tips to get started with neuromarketing—no lab coat needed

Think of it as a journey. We begin with the ancient architecture of the brain, explore how sound, visuals, and multisensory cues create memory, and peek into a future shaped by AI and Neuroscience.

INTRODUCTION

Here's what's inside:

Part 1: "Why Neuromarketing?" — We uncover how the primitive brain drives modern choices and why emotional, energy-saving decisions dominate our behavior.

Part 2: "The Magic of Sound" — From jingles to sonic logos, we explore how sound bypasses logic and hits the heart, embedding brands in memory forever.

Part 3: "Visual Influence" — We dive into how the brain processes and stores visuals and why color, shape, and design consistency matter more than we realize.

Part 4: "The Power of Touch" — Here, we explore how haptics influence brand perception and how a product's texture, shape, or feel impacts memory and value.

Part 5: "Smell & Taste Synergy" — We look at how scent, flavor and taste build emotional recall, and how the fusion of these senses creates unforgettable brand experiences.

Part 6: "Experience Memory" — We understand how all these sensory memories come together to form experience memory and the impact on marketing

Part 7: "The 6Ps and the Brain" — Product, Price, Place, Promotion, People, and Process — all reimagined through the lens of neuroscience.

Part 8: "Marketing Research Reinvented using Neuroscience" — A deep dive into Neurotools — EEG, eye tracking, facial coding, and Implicit Association Tests — and how they outperform traditional research methods.

Part 9: "How "NeuroSensum" is helping Marketers" — We wrap up with how Neurosensum is breaking the frontiers by creating innovative products using AI and Neuroscience to help solve marketing problems

Part 10: "Sensory Brand Audit" — We wrap up by providing a framework for markets to understand what sensory memories they own and what they need to do to create new memory to make their brand appeal to consumers' subconscious brain.

You can read this book from front to back or jump to any section you need. Each chapter is self-contained, but together, they reveal one essential truth:

To truly connect with people, you must understand their brains, not just their words.

So, how should you use this book?

You can use it as a strategic lens before a brand campaign, as inspiration during ideation, or as a refresher before a key pitch. If you're a researcher, dive into the sections on tools and techniques. If you're a creative, focus on the parts about sound, visuals, and multisensory storytelling. If you're a CX leader, lean into the chapters on brand experience and memory formation. Use the insights you gain like tuning forks—helping you create messages, experiences, and moments that resonate with the brain, thereby impacting your brand performance.

Let's begin.

PART 1:
WHY NEUROMARKETING?
Understanding the Subconscious Choice Drivers

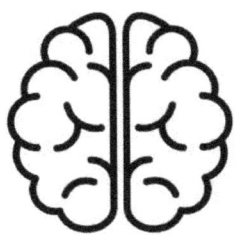

1

THE ANCIENT ENERGY-HUNGRY HUMAN BRAIN

The Ancient Brain
Let's take a moment and go back in time—way back. Imagine standing at an archaeological site, brushing dust off a tool made over 100,000 years ago.

That tool, created by early humans, wasn't fancy. But it got the job done—whether it was hunting, making clothing, or even some form of basic expression. Life was raw, and survival meant keeping things efficient and useful.

Now, here's the twist. Despite all our progress — our smartphones, smart homes, smart everything — the human brain hasn't changed much since those days. It's still wired for survival, still drawn to simplicity, still suspicious of anything too complex. In a way, it's like that multipurpose tool: not flashy, but incredibly efficient when used right.

You see, our brains are around 100,000 years old, and structurally, they've stayed more or less the same since then.

That's because biological evolution is slow, especially when it comes to complex organs like the brain. It takes generations for significant change, and a hundred thousand years isn't as long as it sounds on the evolutionary clock.

At the heart of the brain are three critical structures: the neocortex, the limbic system, and the brainstem. These regions handle everything from emotions to decisions to bodily functions. Since these core functions haven't needed any major upgrades to handle the complexities of modern life, nature hasn't bothered to redesign them. Why fix what isn't broken?

Now, while the brain hasn't evolved biologically, we humans have evolved culturally, and that evolution has been rapid. We've invented languages, built cities, created social networks (both literal and digital), and figured out how to fly across the globe. Yet the core mechanisms our brain uses to process, learn, and decide remain the same.

This creates an interesting dilemma — a mismatch between the ancient wiring of our brain and the hypermodern world we live in. For instance, our brain still craves high-calorie foods because, once upon a time, those were rare and necessary for survival. It's the same with our desire for status, belonging, and security — these instincts are baked into us. This is where things get interesting for marketers. When we talk about appealing to the "old brain," we're essentially trying to communicate in a language the brain already understands, one based on survival, emotion, and instinct.

Take a simple offer like "Buy One Get One Free." That might seem like a basic sales gimmick. But for our ancient brain, it lights up the same reward system that once lit up when we found two mangoes on a tree instead of one. More reward, yet less effort? Yes, please. The key takeaway for marketers is this: We're pitching products and services to a brain that, in evolutionary terms, still thinks it's foraging in the forest. The same brain that once decided which berries to pick now chooses between smartphones.

And that brain still wants the same things—familiarity, simplicity, and reward.

The Energy-Hungry Brain

Let's get one thing straight—the brain may be small, but it's a real energy guzzler.

Even though it makes up just 2 to 3% of our body weight, the brain uses around 20% of our body's total energy. That's huge! It's like running an air conditioner in a room full of candles. And the reason is quite simple: your brain is never off-duty.

Even while you're asleep, daydreaming, or just scrolling your phone mindlessly, your brain is working behind the scenes, managing your body, juggling thoughts, processing memories, and reacting to every tiny sound or sight.

Now, let's break this down a little. Inside your brain are tiny cells called neurons. Think of them as the brain's workers. They're not sitting idle — they're always talking to each other, sending and receiving messages like an endless WhatsApp group chat. This constant activity, especially the electrical signaling between neurons, eats up a lot of energy.

The signaling depends on something called ion gradients—basically, neurons maintain an electrical balance across their membranes by pumping ions in and out, and that process needs a lot of energy. Imagine a battery that's constantly charging and discharging while also sending texts and playing music—that's your brain, all the time.

Then come the synapses—the junctions where one neuron talks to another. Now, here's the crazy part: there are trillions of synapses in your brain. Keeping these connections alive and firing takes an enormous amount of energy. It's like having trillions of phone calls happening at once, 24/7. And if that wasn't enough, the brain is also made up of grey matter, packed with cell bodies and nerve connections. Grey matter is especially active when you're learning something, trying to solve a problem, or just thinking deeply.

Naturally, it demands even more fuel.

Here's the catch: your brain can't store energy like muscles do. It relies entirely on a constant supply of glucose and oxygen from the blood.

If that supply stops, even for a few minutes, the consequences can be fatal. So, the brain is like that fancy car that performs brilliantly but always needs premium fuel—and plenty of it.

But evolution, being its smart operator, came up with a clever counterbalance. If the brain burns through energy like there's no tomorrow, it also works very hard to save energy wherever possible. That's where things like mental shortcuts and habitual behavior come in.

Why the Brain Loves Shortcuts

You know that feeling when you've driven home on autopilot and barely remember the turns? That's your brain saving energy by falling back on habits. It doesn't need to figure out the route daily — it has a shortcut.

This idea of mental shortcuts is central to how our brain handles daily life. In psychology, these are called heuristics, i.e., simple rules or patterns that help us make decisions quickly without using too much mental bandwidth.

Now, this may sound lazy, but it's actually genius. Imagine if your brain had to carefully analyze every email, every menu, every Instagram post, every shopping choice... you'd be exhausted by breakfast. Heuristics are the brain's way of saying, "Let me save you the trouble."

And yes, these shortcuts can sometimes go wrong and lead to biases, but they're still more efficient than overanalyzing everything.

Another thing to note is that the brain has a limited capacity for conscious thinking. It can only focus on a few things at a time, so it tends to filter out anything that feels irrelevant. That's why your brain often favors emotions over logic — feelings are quicker and demand less effort than deep analysis.

Also, our brain loves familiarity. It leans heavily on past experiences when making decisions.

Even if it's not the most rational choice, going with what "feels right" is often more energy efficient.

That's what we call a gut feeling, and it's often just your brain reaching into its archive of memories.

Now, think about how often we simplify decisions by turning them into binary options—yes or no, buy or don't, like or skip. This is the brain trying to avoid cognitive overload. However, if it has to make too many decisions in a row, it becomes tired. This is what we call decision fatigue—and it's very real. After a long day, even choosing what to eat can feel like a major task.

This insight into the energy-hungry brain opens up powerful possibilities for marketing.

If you want someone to make a decision, make it easy. Reduce the effort. Remove friction. Offer choices, but not too many. Use familiar and emotionally resonant visuals and words.

If the brain finds something comforting, efficient, or habit-forming, it'll take to it like fish to water. That's why things like default settings, emotional storytelling, and consistent brand cues work so well.

And when you understand that even your most "rational" customers are making decisions based on what feels familiar, fast, or emotionally satisfying, you change the entire way you approach communication.

The brain's hunger for energy might be intense, but so is its need to protect and preserve itself. Marketing, when done right, respects this balance. It aligns with how the brain actually works rather than how we think it *should* work.

Heuristics and Shortcuts: A Case Study

We're bringing in our friend Sarah now.

Now, Sarah is a sharp, driven marketing executive living in a fast-moving metropolitan city. She's someone who juggles deadlines, meetings, personal errands, and about a thousand tiny decisions every single day.

You probably know someone like Sarah, someone in your life who seems to buzz around the office like a bee aiming to pollinate every flower in the garden.

Always on top of her game and somehow always a step ahead. But what really keeps her going isn't just her to-do list or the regularly filled coffee cup that sits on her desk. Instead, the one that should be getting those flowers is none other than her brain. Her brain has the knack for doing one smart thing again and again: taking shortcuts. Now, we're not talking about shortcuts in a lazy way. That word has done disastrous things to people's vocabulary. Shortcuts can be clever and, many times, necessary. These are smart survival tactics and what neuroscience calls heuristics.

They can be considered mental "rules-of-thumb" our brains use to cut through clutter and make decisions as quickly and efficiently as possible. In today's world, where every waking minute bombards us with choices, heuristics is how our brain pushes everything aside and goes, "Let's not waste energy on that today."

So, let's take a look at a day in Sarah's life and see how these shortcuts work.

1. The Morning Hustle

Sarah wakes up 30 minutes late. There's no time to think. She reaches into her wardrobe and picks out a go-to outfit. Why that one? Simple. Her brain already tagged it as "professional + comfortable." No debate required. That's a heuristic in action — a connection forged through repeated use.

As she rushes out, she avoids her daily café because she knows it would have a long line and heads to a smaller one around the corner. Her brain remembers that the coffee there is just as good and the service is faster. That's the *availability heuristic*—quickly relying on recent, positive experiences.

2. At Work

By 10 AM, as she sits down to work, Sarah's inbox looks like a battlefield. Unread emails and numbers fill up her screen everywhere.

But she's not panicking, no, that would be inefficient.

Instead, she immediately scans the messages for familiar names and important subject lines and skips the rest (for the time being, of course).

That's what is called the *recognition heuristic*. If her brain knows it, it assumes it's important. Later, she sits with her team in the boardroom discussing influence partnerships. On the screen, multiple profiles are being analyzed for the pick, but Sarah instantly vouches for a well-known public figure. Why? Her brain uses the *"halo effect,"* a shortcut where one positive trait (fame) gets extended to assume other traits (credibility, trustworthiness). Deep research can come later. For now, she trusts her gut.

3. Decision Time

In the afternoon, she sits at her desk, burdened with another choice. This time, she has to choose between two creative campaigns. The first one has impressive data stacked in it, but it feels too dry and unemotional. The second one has a more engaging and emotional narrative. So, Sarah decides that she's going to go with the one that "feels right."

That's the *affect heuristic*—where feelings lead the decision. She may return to the data later and find another decision that seems more logical, but at that moment, her emotional "gut feelings" drive the call. And neuroscience tells us that emotional decisions often present themselves as faster and easier.

4. Wrapping Up the Day

By evening, Sarah finally gets back home. Tired and too drained to cook, she instinctively opens a food delivery app and orders sushi. You may wonder, why sushi? Well, it's probably because she passed a billboard featuring sushi on her way back home. That's the priming effect—a subtle influence that left a visual trace in her subconscious.

What This Tells Us About the Brain

There's definitely something you've noticed from this sequence of events. None of Sarah's decisions were random or careless.

Each choice contributed to her efficiency, allowing her to conserve mental energy while navigating life with minimal cognitive strain. Just as we function, her brain was doing its best to keep her focused on the more important and taxing tasks by streamlining the less important ones.

It perfectly aligns with the tendency to go "autopilot," when you end up defaulting to the "typically selected" choices.

But, as there is for most things, there's a flip side. Sometimes, shortcuts tend to be biased. We ignore better options, rely too much on past patterns, or let emotions override logic. That's the trade-off for fast decision-making. In a world overloaded with stimuli, our brain ends up picking "fast" and "good enough" over "slow and perfect" almost every time. This is probably to prevent itself from getting overwhelmed.

How do these relate to NeuroMarketing?

If you're in marketing, here's your golden insight: consumers are not making decisions with spreadsheets. They react based on what feels familiar, easy, emotionally safe, or socially validated.

So this means your job isn't just to present information. Your job is to make your brand the default choice. The more you align your strategy with how the brain actually works, the more naturally your brand will fit into people's lives, just like it did for our buddy Sarah.

Then comes the big old question: How are all these related to neuromarketing? We've talked about how the mind saves energy and expends so much energy even in the most mundane tasks. So, how does marketing actually take advantage of this? Can it?

Enter center stage: **Neuromarketing**.

The very essence of neuromarketing lies in aligning your strategies with how the human brain naturally thinks, feels, and makes decisions. Calling it manipulations puts a bad taste in everyone's mouths; it's more like studying the waves before you ride them. Let's start by understanding at the most basic level.

System 1 vs System 2 Thinking

Nobel Prize-winning psychologist Daniel Kahneman introduced the world to System 1 and System 2 thinking.
- System 1 is fast, intuitive, emotional, and automatic.
- System 2 is slow, analytical, effortful, and deliberate.

Most marketing, whether we admit it or not, targets System 1, as this is what consumers rely on most often. They're not analyzing every feature or comparing every statistic. Instead, they choose what feels right, what they've encountered before, and what captures their emotional attention.

Consider the last time you selected a biscuit brand from the shelf. Did you examine the price per gram and compare the nutritional information? Probably not. You recognized a familiar brand, perhaps a flavor you enjoy, and made your decision in just two seconds. That's System 1 in action. The job of neuromarketing is to design for that fast, automatic, emotional brain.

What Marketers Can Do (Using the Brain's Rules)

Let's explore a few ways neuroscience and marketing overlap, and how you can use these ideas in real marketing action plans.

1. Emotional Responses – The Heart Still Rules

Emotions aren't just those feelings of happiness or sadness that you feel; they're deeply tied to decision-making. The limbic system, especially the amygdala[3] and hippocampus, lights up like a bulb when something makes us feel something. If your ad can evoke any range of emotions like happiness, nostalgia, excitement, or even surprise, it's already halfway into the customer's long-term memory. And if your storytelling can trigger empathy, you've formed a connection that logic alone can't beat. So, whether it's a feel-good ad, a tearjerker, or even a playful jingle, it sticks if it stirs a feeling.

2. Subconscious Shortcuts & Choice Architecture

Remember heuristics? Those energy-saving rules the brain relies on? Marketers use them all the time—sometimes without even realizing it. One big one is framing. The way a choice is presented can influence what people choose.

For example, a "90% fat-free" label sounds better than "10% fat," even though they're the same thing. Then there's the Paradox of Choice. Give people too many options, and their brain freezes, and that's what we call decision paralysis. That's why curated, limited options often perform better. It's easier on the brain.

A good marketer becomes a kind of architect for decisions—arranging the environment to guide, not push.

3. Sensory Marketing – Make the Brain Feel the Brand

Our brains are built for multi-sensory experiences. When brands engage multiple senses: sight, sound, touch, and even smell, they tap into a deeper kind of memory storage.

- Think of the crunch of a chip in a Lay's ad.
- The fizz of cola.
- The velvety application of a luxury skincare ad.

These are not just a visual; they aim to be immersive. That's what makes them memorable. Also, there's something called *Sensory Specific Satiation*, which is a fancy way of saying we get bored easily.

Variation in textures, flavors, visuals—even ad formats—can keep consumers engaged for longer.

4. Storytelling – The Brain's Favorite Format

We humans are wired for stories—and always have been. From bedtime tales to Netflix binges, stories have always been a method of helping us make sense of the world. In marketing, storytelling triggers *narrative transportation* — a state where the consumer feels like they're *inside* the story. That's when persuasion is at its strongest. But it's not just about emotion, it's also about coherence.

How much does it make sense to the brain? How easily conveyed is the core message? Does the brain have to work a lot to understand the themes? If your message is clear, consistent, and easy to follow, the brain will love it.

Confusion = Rejection; Simplicity = Retention. Ditch the jargon and focus on clarity, flow, and relatability.

5. Social Proof & Authority– Herd Instinct, Activated

Human beings are social creatures. We follow the crowd. We listen to authority. Why? Because it's safer. Evolution trained us that way. So when your marketing shows that "Everyone's using it" or "Experts recommend it," you're speaking directly to that ancient part of the brain that says, "If others trust it, maybe I should too." This is why influencer marketing, testimonials, and celebrity endorsements work so well—they shortcut trust.

6. Cognitive Biases– The Brain's Quirky Rules

Let's end with a few powerful biases that marketers love (and for good reason):

- **Anchoring:** The first number or idea you show becomes a reference point. Show a higher price first, and the sale price feels like a steal.
- **Loss Aversion:** People hate losing more than they enjoy gaining. So instead of "Buy now and save ₹500," try "Don't miss out on ₹500 in savings."

These aren't tricks, they're just predictable brain behaviors. And when used ethically, they can make marketing more human and more effective.

Wrapping It Up– Neuromarketing Is Just Smart Marketing

Neuromarketing isn't some manipulative tool—it's about understanding human nature. It's recognizing that we're still driven by ancient instincts, emotional reactions, and energy-saving shortcuts beneath all our devices, data, and digital lives. So, whether you're writing a headline, designing a product, or launching a campaign, keep this in mind: You're not marketing to a machine. You're speaking to a 100,000-year-old brain that still responds best to emotion, simplicity, familiarity, and reward. Get that right, and you won't just get clicks or conversions—you'll get a connection to your consumers.

2

MOMENTS OF TRUTH AND BRAND MEMORY

The Journey of a Decision – One Moment at a Time

Think about the last time you purchased something—not a small, everyday item, but a decision that made you pause. Maybe something major like a washing machine. Or something in need of meticulous research, like a new pair of headphones. Or even a skincare product. Chances are, you didn't just wake up and hit "Buy Now." Whether you realize it or not, your brain went through a sequence of moments—each one shaping the final decision.

Marketers call these "Moments of Truth." Neuroscience shows us that each of these moments creates a memory—a tiny impression that can tip the scales later.

Let's examine how this plays out, not in theory but in a realistic way. Let's follow Kanchana.

Kanchana's Story: A Journey Through Moments of Truth

Kanchana is a sharp and practical teacher. After years of loyal service, her trusty old washing machine suddenly broke down one day. No big drama, but she knows she needs a replacement soon.

ZMOT: The Zero Moment of Truth

That evening, sitting on her couch, tablet in hand, Kanchana starts researching. "Best washing machines for large families," she types in. She scrolls through reviews, blog posts, and YouTube comparisons. She remembers her friend Sofia raving about her new model just a few months ago. And then there's her own positive memory of the previous brand, which lasted a solid eight years.

At this point, Kanchana isn't ready to buy. She's just gathering impressions—subconsciously building mental associations.

This is what Google calls the Zero Moment of Truth (ZMOT)—the phase when a consumer begins forming opinions even before interacting with the brand directly. In fact, I'd go a step further and say ZMOT starts even when we're not planning to buy—when we pass a billboard, see a video, or overhear a conversation. The brain stores it all.

For marketers, this is the quietest but most powerful moment. It's not the time to hard-sell. It's the time to seed curiosity, emotion, and value.

FMOT: The First Moment of Truth

A few days later, Kanchana finally visits an appliance store. There are rows of washing machines, but one seems to stand out. It's from the same brand she read about and remembered from her friend's story. The display is clear, the energy ratings are impressive, and there's an added bonus: *it's on an exchange offer.*

This is the First Moment of Truth (FMOT), a term coined by Procter & Gamble. It's the exact point when the consumer encounters the product, whether on the shelf or online.

And let me tell you, this moment is brutally short. It takes just 3 to 7 seconds to make a lasting impression.

The brain quickly evaluates: "Do I like this? Is it familiar? Do I trust it?" That's why everything—design, layout, colour, label, CTA—matters here. The emotional brain does most of the heavy lifting in those few seconds. If the product doesn't connect here, the sale might be lost forever.

SMOT: The Second Moment of Truth

Kanchana decides to buy it. She takes it home, sets it up, and uses it the next day. It's quiet, quick, and gets the job done beautifully. She smiles, satisfied. Her brain now has a clear "yes" impression stored.

This is the Second Moment of Truth (SMOT)—when the consumer actually uses the product. This moment can confirm or contradict everything the brain believed during ZMOT and FMOT.

There's something even more interesting from neuroscience: when the brain has a good experience, it tags it for the future. So the next time Kanchana needs a kitchen appliance or gives a recommendation, that memory becomes the shortcut. No overthinking, just a familiar, trusted choice.

If the experience is average? The brain forgets. If it's poor? The brain remembers—scarily vividly. Marketers need to take advantage of that emotional weight of product experience.

Abhishek's Everyday Encounters: Brand Memory in Real Life

Now let's look at another example— Abhishek, a busy working professional. His day starts with a slight disappointment: the recently bought smart coffee machine stops working. That moment is stored. A negative SMOT.

He hops on his electric scooter, which he's been using for months without issues. That consistent performance reinforces a positive brand memory. At work, he's fed up with office noise and begins researching noise-cancelling headphones during his lunch break. He's now in his ZMOT—browsing reviews, comparing prices, remembering what a friend recommended.

What's fascinating here is that these micro-moments constantly build associations in Abhishek's mind. He's not sitting with a spreadsheet doing pros and cons. He's absorbing cues, storing emotions, and forming shortcuts without realizing it. And later, when it's time actually to buy something, his brain calls up these stored memories to guide the choice.

The Brain's Memory System: Where Brand Encounters Live

Every time we experience a brand—whether through sight, sound, touch, or use—the brain kicks into gear. It begins encoding that stimulus using different memory systems:

- Visual cues go to the occipital lobe
- Sounds are processed in the temporal lobe[12]
- Emotions light up the amygdala[3]
- Motor actions (like using the product) trigger the cerebellum
- And finally, the hippocampus decides if the experience is worth storing long-term

When multiple senses are engaged, like sight, sound, and emotion, the memory formed in that moment is reinforced. For example, if you look at your own life, you may notice that you can't actively recall and remember the mundane day-to-day events of your life. Still, you can easily remember an experience you had when you were young and got really scared, like when you broke a vase or rolled down some stairs. This is why multisensory branding works so well. It lights up more areas of the brain.

Neuroplasticity – Why Repetition Matters So Much

The brain isn't fixed. Thanks to neuroplasticity, it's always adapting—rewiring itself based on experience.

For marketers, every ad, product interaction, and brand touchpoint can strengthen a neural pathway.

- When Nike says "Just Do It" again and again, they're carving a groove in your brain.

- When a brand delivers a consistent emotional experience, it becomes easier to recall—and harder to ignore.

This is how habits are formed, too. Cue + reward = routine. If a product becomes part of someone's daily routine, their brain stops questioning it and just accepts it as the default. Brands that understand this can train consumer behavior over time, not by shouting louder but by consistently showing up emotionally and across multiple senses. It could be a jingle, a smell in a store, a packaging texture, or the experience of using the product itself. The brain processes it all, and depending on how strong or emotional that experience was, it decides whether to store it or discard it.

Implication for Marketers

Here are some ways in which marketers can create and strengthen brand memories by using Neuroplasticity:

1. Brand Associations Get Stronger with Repetition

The more frequently a consumer sees or hears a brand element, such as a slogan, a color, or a sound, the stronger the connection becomes. It's very similar to the idea of "desire paths," the trails formed by humans for a variety of reasons, but most often to avoid using the longer and more exhaustive pathways laid out. The more people who cut through the grass instead of circling the grass, the clearer the path becomes. Similarly, your brand becomes more memorable with each exposure.

2. Brands Can Help Form Habits

By creating consistent cues and rewards, marketers can actually train the brain to form routines. Think of a daily skincare brand that shows up with a reminder every morning and night. Over time, the brand becomes part of the consumer's mental autopilot.

3. Emotionally Charged Ads Leave Stronger Imprints

When your marketing stirs emotion—be it laughter, nostalgia, pride, or even sadness—it activates the amygdala[3], which in turn strengthens memory consolidation. That's why ads that make us feel tend to stick more than ones that just present facts.

4. Marketing Can Educate the Brain

Instructional content, such as explainer videos, how-to reels, and infographics, doesn't just provide the brain with information. It also creates new neural pathways, especially when repeated or paired with visual cues. That's how consumer perception can be shaped over time.

5. Multisensory Inputs Build Robust Brand Memory

Sight + sound + texture + smell = deeper brain engagement. The more senses you activate, the more areas of the brain you engage.

This is why luxury brands often invest in signature scents, tactile packaging, and rich sound design. Long story short: neural plasticity is why your brand can become unforgettable—if you consistently and emotionally repeat the right messages in the right way.

Let's go a step further. Once a brand enters the brain, how does it stay there? How is it recalled during that critical buying moment?

The brain works through associative memory, a web where one stimulus triggers another.

This nature of memory might make the smell of sandalwood remind you of your grandfather, or the sound of temple bells bring back memories of Diwali mornings. Brands can, and should, become part of this network of associations.

Types of Brand Memory – Stored in Different Brain Zones

Here's a simple list of the different types of memory relevant for marketers and how they are stored in different parts of the brain.:

1. Visual Memory – "I recognize that logo."

Housed in the occipital lobe, colors, shapes, fonts, and packaging trigger visual memory. That's why a brand's visual identity must be consistent. Think Coca-Cola red, Apple white, or McDonald's yellow arches.

2. Sonic Memory – "I know that sound!"

Stored in the temporal lobe[12], this involves sound cues like jingles, notification sounds, voiceovers, and music. Sonic branding isn't optional anymore—it's a shortcut to instant recognition.

3. Experience Memory – "I've used it, and it worked well."

Formed through direct product interaction, it is stored across multiple systems, particularly in the hippocampus (for long-term memory) and the cerebellum (for physical and motor tasks). A good or bad experience stays with the user and influences future choices.

4. Emotional Memory – "It made me feel something."

The amygdala[3] stores emotions, especially those linked to safety, pleasure, fear, or nostalgia. Emotional experiences with a brand—whether through stories, ads, or actual usage—can create loyalty that logic can't shake.

5. Image Memory – "This brand feels smart, cool, or premium."

This goes beyond visuals—it's about the overall brand personality. If a brand is always associated with clean design, intelligent communication, and innovation, the brain assigns it a "smart" image, which plays a huge role in brand preference.

6. User Imagery Memory – "People like me use this."

This memory is shaped by who we see using the product—celebrities, influencers, neighbors, even ourselves. The brain creates a shortcut: "This product fits people like me." It can even be turned into the inverse, where your brain suddenly associates using the product with attaining what the user has (status, looks, weight). It's often what drives aspirational buying.

7. Sensory Memory – "I remember how it smells, feels, or sounds."

Sensory memories are compelling, stored in areas like the olfactory bulb and somatosensory cortex. One signature scent in a store can become brand DNA. Textures, packaging clicks, and even product weight can leave lasting impressions.

8. Value and Price Memory – "It's worth the money."

This includes perceived value for money, deals, and premium cues stored in association networks involving reward and evaluation systems. Anchoring plays a significant role here (remember that first price the brain sees?).

Why Brand Memory Is the Marketer's Goldmine

All these types of memory come together to form what we call brand equity or brand DNA, i.e., the intangible strength your brand carries in the consumer's mind.

Strong brand memories can:
- Shorten decision-making time
- Increase repeat purchases
- Make consumers less price-sensitive
- Drive referrals and recommendations

And the most powerful part? These memories are formed quietly, emotionally, and often subconsciously.

Make Your Brand Worth Remembering

You don't need to shout to be remembered. You need to engage the brain the way it prefers—through emotion, repetition, sensory richness, and clear storytelling. When your brand becomes part of someone's memory, it stops being a product. It becomes a familiar feeling. A shortcut. A safe choice And in a world full of noise, the brands that win are the ones that don't just compete for attention—they become part of memory.

PART 2:
THE MAGIC OF SOUND
Why What You Hear Stays With You

3

DECODING SONIC MEMORY

Let's start with a simple question.

Have you ever heard a tune from your childhood—maybe from an old TV show, a wedding band, or a dusty radio—and suddenly found yourself smiling? Or crying? Or just... transported somewhere else entirely?

That, my friends, is the power of sound. It doesn't knock politely like a guest. It walks straight into your heart, settles down comfortably, and makes itself at home.

Now, let's rewind— sound was present way before there were words, even before humans managed to come up with anything like alphabets, scripts, or even fire. In those wild, unpredictable forests where early humans lived, sound was everything. A snap of a twig might mean danger. The rush of a river meant water. A low growl from the bushes? You didn't wait to investigate—you ran.

You see, hearing wasn't just one of our senses. It was our survival system. Our ancestors weren't just strong or clever; they had ears tuned like radar. And this sensitivity to sound—this deep, biological dependency—has never left us. We've just buried it under layers of modern life. But sound...it always remembers.

Unlike images, which the brain has to decode—figure out the shape, the depth, the colour—sound is immediate. It takes the express route to the limbic system, where your emotions live. There's no security check, no baggage scanning. Sound walks right in and presses buttons you didn't even know existed.

It's why a baby's cry can make your chest ache. Or why that ringtone from your ex's number can twist your stomach before your brain even registers who's calling.

This is the doing of a little almond-shaped structure in the brain called the amygdala[3]. Think of it as your emotional smoke detector. It's old, primitive, and fast. And sound triggers it in milliseconds. Literally. The brain processes sound in as little as 10 milliseconds—before you can blink, before you can think.

Vision? That's the complicated cousin. It has to flip the image upside down on your retina, sort colors, adjust for depth... it's elegant but slow. Sound, on the other hand, is raw instinct.

Let's be fair, sight is beautiful. Paintings, sunsets, cinema—all visual poetry. But sound? Sound is a feeling.

Think of this: A photograph of your school might remind you of your school days. But the school bell? That takes you back, doesn't it? Suddenly, you're standing in a dusty corridor, uniform that was always a little too tight, waiting for that final bell to run home.

That's sonic memory. It doesn't ask for permission. It just opens the door and takes you on a ride.

And unlike visuals, sound doesn't demand your attention. You can be driving, cooking, or scrolling through Instagram, and still, music, podcasts, or background noise can slip into your subconscious. This makes sound an unsung hero in our overstimulated world. It fits in where sight can't.

The Brain's Hidden Recorder

Now here's something fascinating: sound doesn't just enter and vanish. Your brain, clever as it is, has a sort of internal audio playback system. Neuroscientists call it echoic memory.

It's like a mental voice recorder that captures sounds for a few seconds long enough to figure out what's important.

You hear a door creak. Your brain stores that creak for a beat or two, just in case it matters. Was it the wind? A cat? Or... something else? Your conscious mind is still catching up while your subconscious is already preparing a reaction.

And the beauty? You don't even have to be actively listening. Your brain is always, *always* listening. Even when your eyes are elsewhere, your ears are on high alert. This passive listening system is what makes sound so powerful in marketing, storytelling, and memory-making.

The Emotional Chemistry of Sound

Let's go deeper. Why does music make us cry? Or dance? Or feel brave?

It's chemistry, really. When you listen to a song you love, your brain releases dopamine—the pleasure molecule. If it's nostalgic, you might also get a dose of serotonin for that warm, fuzzy feeling. Sad songs?

They might trigger prolactin, a hormone that soothes emotional pain. Isn't that poetic? The brain has a way to hold your hand when you're hurting.

This is why music therapy works. It's not just "feel good" fluff—it's biologically backed healing. Sound quite literally helps regulate your mood, your stress, and your heartbeat.

You don't just listen to music. Your body feels it.

Let's shift gears for a second.

If sound has this kind of access to our memory and emotions, don't you think it's an absolute goldmine for marketers? A catchy jingle, a warm voiceover, a familiar notification sound—they can become a part of your daily life without you even realizing it.

That's the power of sonic branding. It doesn't just tell you about a brand—it makes you *feel* the brand. Think of the Netflix "ta-dum." Or the Intel bong. Or, closer to home, the Titan tune.

You don't have to see the logo. That sound *is* the brand. In a world where our eyes are exhausted from too much screen time, ears are the new frontier. And the brands that understand this are already way ahead. Before we learned to speak, we cooed.

Before alphabets, we sang lullabies. And even now, a baby in any part of the world will respond to rhythm and tone before it understands a single word. Sound is ancient. It's sacred. And it's intimate. It's what connects us—not just to each other, but to our own memories, feelings, and stories.

In the end, sound doesn't need to shout to be heard. Sometimes, the softest note carries the deepest emotion. And in this noisy world, be heard if you want to be remembered.

4

SONIC BRANDING: THE MUSIC OF YOUR BRAND

Let me ask you something.
When you hear *"I'm lovin' it..."* can you stop your brain from singing the rest? Or when someone hums that Titan jingle, don't you instantly picture class, elegance, and maybe a gift wrapped for someone special?

That, right there, is sonic branding at its finest.

You see, in a world flooded with visuals—logos, fonts, colors—sound is that quiet genius in the background, working its charm, seeping into your subconscious, and building emotional real estate for a brand, without even asking for your permission.

A good sonic identity is not just a tune—it's a memory shortcut. A key that opens a whole drawer full of feelings, visuals, and stories in your brain. Neuroscientists have a lovely term for this: neurological iconic signature.

Let's break it down simply. Every time you hear a brand's audio cue—say, the soft "ta-dum" of Netflix or the confident chime of Intel—your brain doesn't just say "ah yes, Netflix." It often recalls when you last binged your favorite series, or how that sound meant winding down after a long day.

That's what this signature does. It's not just branding. It's anchoring.

And when that sound becomes familiar—predictable even—it doesn't just inform. It comforts. In a strange, chaotic world, that tiny sonic moment becomes... home.

Jingles: The Anthems of Ads

Now, who doesn't love a good jingle?

Catchy, short, and often cheesy in the best possible way, jingles have a way of latching on to your brain like a happy little parasite. And they don't let go.

Remember:
- *"Washing powder Nirma..."*
- *"Vicco Turmeric, nahi cosmetic..."*
- Or the anthem of every office-goer who's had a KitKat: *"Give me a break..."*

These aren't just tunes. They are *emotional time machines*.

What makes jingles so sticky? A mix of rhythm, melody, and repetition. But more importantly, they work because they feel familiar, almost like a nursery rhyme. You hum them in the shower, whistle them in traffic, and sometimes, they just pop into your head uninvited.

Over time, they don't just help recall a brand. They *become* the brand.

Audio Logos: Small Sounds, Big Impressions

Now, think of the Netflix "ta-dum." Or the Apple boot-up chime. These are not full songs, but they carry weight. They're like the tiniest nudge that says, "Hey, it's us again."

That's an audio logo—the sound equivalent of a visual logo.

Just a few seconds, but enough to build recognition, identity, even trust.

The key here? Two things:

1. Consistency – play the same sound across every touchpoint.
2. Duration – keep it short and snappy.

No one wants to hear a mini opera before a YouTube ad.

Some classic examples:
- Intel's five-note bong? Feels like innovation.
- Airtel's jingle by A.R. Rahman? Sounds like connectivity wrapped in emotion.
- Britannia's "Ting ting ti ting"? Pure joy.
- Tokopedia's comforting "To-ko-pe-dia" tune.

Audio logos work best when they become muscle memory. You don't think about them. You *feel* them.

The Titan Story: An Indian Masterclass in Sonic Branding

Ah, Titan. Now this one deserves a slow clap.

Imagine this: back in the late '80s, Titan chose Mozart's Symphony No. 25 as its brand tune. Western classical music was hardly mainstream in India back then. But it worked. Oh, it *worked*.

Why?

Because they didn't just use a tune, they wove emotion into it. Love. Gifting. Elegance. Time. All packed into that sweeping melody. Over the years, they tweaked it with Indian instruments, layered it into ads that celebrated women, relationships, and moments.

They didn't just market watches. They told stories with music as the narrator.

And now, that Titan tune? It's not just a sound. It's an emotion. You hear it and you remember birthdays, anniversaries, and those tiny, priceless moments you marked with a gift.

That's sonic branding at its highest form—when a brand doesn't just sell, but *belongs*.

Licensed Music: When Familiar Tunes Do the Heavy Lifting

Sometimes, brands borrow a tune that already lives in your emotional archive. This is called licensed music, where brands pay to use popular songs in ads.

And why not? Music already loved by millions carries instant emotional value.

Remember these?

- Apple used *Chariots of Fire* to position the Macintosh as a revolution.
- Nike paired *Revolution* by The Beatles with visuals of courage and energy.
- Coca-Cola India breathed life into *"Tum Jo Mil Gaye Ho"* for its "togetherness" campaigns.
- Google's Reunion ad used *"Ajeeb Dastan Hai Yeh"* to make us cry with joy (you know the one, right?).

And in India, Bollywood songs? Gold. Nostalgia. Melody. Culture. All rolled into one. From Airtel's "Har Ek Friend Zaroori Hota Hai" to MakeMyTrip's "Dil Hai Chhota Sa", licensed music becomes emotional shorthand. It's a strategic shortcut from brand to heart.

Product Sounds: Every Click, Sizzle, and Fizz Matters

Ever noticed how satisfying the crunch of a potato chip sounds in a Lays ad? Or that fizz when a soda can pops open? Well, let me tell you, those are all intentional.

These are engineered sounds, part of a brand's sonic experience, which is vital to selling their product. Luxury car makers obsess over how their car door sounds when it shuts. It has to be *thunk*, not *thud*. That's how we're trained to associate sound with craftsmanship.

Smartphone companies showcase the sound of the camera shutter to promise clarity. Coffee ads linger over the pouring of liquid or the sizzling of food to spark your taste buds and get that saliva pooling.

THE MAGIC OF SOUND

So, the next time you and your team are brainstorming any branding ideas, remember—your logo may be seen. Your tagline may be read. But your sound? That will be felt.

Because sometimes, the best way to be remembered is to be heard.

The 4 Types of Sonic Branding

So now that we've walked through the beautiful world of sonic branding, let's get into the nitty-gritty. Not all sounds in branding are created equal. It's like Indian music—ragas, film songs, bhajans, and folk tunes. Each serves a purpose and touches a different part of you.

In the same way, there are four powerful types of sonic branding, each playing its own role in how a brand speaks to your soul.

Let's break them down one by one—with a bit of rhythm, nostalgia, and insight.

1. Jingles – The Catchy Companions

If sound were food, jingles would be street food —spicy, quick, unforgettable.

A jingle is a catchy song that sticks in your mind. You hear it once, and two hours later, you're still humming it while brushing your teeth. That's precisely the idea. It's musical glue.

Usually, jingles carry the brand name or a message wrapped in rhythm and melody that's designed to go viral in your brain.

Think of:
- *"Washing Powder Nirma..."*
- *"Vicco Turmeric, nahi cosmetic..."*
- *"Give me a break, break me off a piece of that Kit-Kat bar..."*

These aren't just ad tools. They're generational memories. They've become part of our lives, allowing us to randomly sing the first few words and know that our friends will join in instantly, with the eagerness of a child.

The real power of a jingle lies in how it blends emotion + recall.

You may forget the ad, but you'll remember the tune.

And decades later, it can still transport you to your childhood living room, watching Doordarshan with your family. Brands that get this right stay with you for life.

2. Audio Logos – Small but Mighty

Now, let's discuss the refined relative of the jingle: the audio logo. If a jingle is a complete meal, then an audio logo is like that distinct spice—concise, sharp, and instantly identifiable. Brands across various touchpoints utilize these small, iconic sounds. Typically lasting just 2 to 5 seconds, they can leave a lasting impact. Examples?

- Intel's iconic "bong bong bong bong bong" – innovation in a few notes.
- Netflix's "ta-dum" – a prelude to your binge session.
- Airtel's melody – emotion wrapped in sound and crafted by A.R. Rahman himself.
- Britannia's "ting ting ti ting" – light, joyful, unforgettable.

What makes audio logos powerful?

- Consistency: They appear everywhere—TV, Apps, YouTube, even in-store.
- Simplicity: They're not cluttered. It just has a few seconds of sound, but it is distinct.

Over time, these sounds become similar to reflex reactions. When you hear them, your brain says, "Oh, I know who that is." You don't need visuals. You don't need context. The sound becomes its own identity.

3. Licensed Music – Borrowing Emotion, Instantly

Sometimes, a brand doesn't create a sound—it borrows one. And that's not cheating. That's strategy.

Licensed music is when brands use existing, popular songs in their ads. Why? Because these songs already carry emotional baggage—good baggage. They already mean something to you. So the brand doesn't have to build emotion from scratch—it just taps into what's already there.

Let's look at some brilliant cases:
- Apple used *Chariots of Fire* in its "1984" ad. Epic. Revolutionary.
- Nike went with *Revolution* by The Beatles—perfect for a brand about breaking boundaries.
- Microsoft used *Beautiful Day* by U2—technology meets optimism.
- Google India used *Ajeeb Dastan Hai Yeh* in its partition reunion ad. Try watching that without a lump in your throat.

And in India, Bollywood music is a goldmine:
- MakeMyTrip used *"Dil Hai Chhota Sa"* to capture youthful wanderlust.
- Airtel created a whole new song—*"Har Ek Friend Zaroori Hota Hai"*—that became a friendship anthem.
- Coca-Cola reimagined *"Tum Jo Mil Gaye Ho"* to promote togetherness. Chilled drink, warm emotions.

Licensed music is a shortcut to the heart.

When used right, it amplifies your brand's message with the power of shared cultural memory.

4. Product Sounds – Function Meets Feeling

Now here's a sneaky one—product sounds. These are the natural, often engineered sounds from the product.

But don't let the simplicity fool you. These are sonic goldmines.

Let's take a few examples:
- The *click* of a luxury car door closing—it sounds expensive.
- The *fizz* of a Coke being poured over ice—instant thirst.
- The *shutter click* of a phone camera says, "You're capturing something special."
- The *crunch* of a chip in a Lays ad—crispy perfection.

- The *sizzle* of a burger on a McDonald's grill—hunger switch: ON.

These aren't just sounds. They're telling you something about the product: it's premium, it's tasty, it's reliable, it's exciting.

In today's world of ASMR (Autonomous Sensory Meridian Response), brands are leaning even more into this. Whispered ads, close-up sounds, intimate tones—all crafted to make you feel, not just hear.

You see, sonic branding isn't just about being loud. It's about being memorable. Each of these four types—jingles, audio logos, licensed music, and product sounds—has its own flavor. And together, they create a rich, textured identity for a brand.

One that you don't just recognize... but feel. Because at the end of the day, people aren't coming in just for the products.

They're trying to buy the experience they saw in that ad, whether it's the clean-cut gentleman look they see in Raymonds or the spotless, professional, and stark white shirt that Tide promises. Sound, dear reader, is one of the most potent ways to make someone instantly and deeply feel something.

5

DEVELOPING A SONIC IDENTITY — CRAFT YOUR BRAND'S VOICE

Imagine your brand as a person. How would they sound? Would they be bold like a dhol at a Punjabi wedding? Or subtle and sophisticated like a flute playing in the background of a quiet art gallery?

That's where sonic identity begins. It's not just about choosing a nice tune. It's about finding a voice. A sound that doesn't stop at speaking to your customer's ears. A sound that feels like you.

Developing a sonic identity isn't guesswork, it's more of a journey—a bit like composing a raga. You need structure, intuition, and a deep understanding of who you're playing for.

Let's walk through that journey step by step.

Step 1: Know Thyself (and Thy Brand)
Before you pick a note, you need to know the soul behind the song.

A. Core Values – What Do You Stand For?

What are your brand's non-negotiables? Integrity, Innovation, Joy, or Simplicity?

These values guide your business strategy and shape your sound. A tech startup pushing innovation might lean toward futuristic, electronic tones. A heritage tea brand? Maybe soft sitar, earthy textures, and a slow rhythm. Your sound needs to mirror exactly what you hope the customer will feel.

B. Brand Personality – What Party Personality Are You?

Is your brand quirky and playful? Or maybe elegant and refined?

This personality should drip into your sonic choices. Tempo, pitch, and tonality are all brushstrokes in your audio portrait. For a young, energetic brand, opt for an upbeat and catchy tone. For a premium brand, consider a slower tempo, richer textures, and perhaps orchestral tones.

Your sound should embody and reflect the essence of your brand.

C. Emotions – What Do You Want People to Feel?

This is a big one.

Do you want people to feel excitement? Trust? Nostalgia? Empowerment?

Sound is an emotional conductor. Music psychologists know this well—minor scales evoke sadness, fast rhythms spark energy, drones build tension, and harmonies create calm.

So, choose wisely. You're not just choosing what your brand says—you're choosing how it makes people feel.

Step 2: KYA (Know Your Audience)

Now let's flip the spotlight. Who are you playing for?

A. Demographics – Age, Gender, Income

Young adults might respond to edgy, global beats. Older consumers? Perhaps melodies with a touch of tradition. A Gen Z audience may vibe with trap or lo-fi. A wellness audience might lean towards soothing nature sounds or acoustic strings.

B. Culture – This One's Big in India

A sound that works in Tokyo may fall flat in Tamil Nadu.

Cultural nuances are everything. In India, for instance, the tabla and bansuri might evoke a sense of comfort and rootedness, while EDM or synth music might convey a feeling of modernity. What's "premium" in one market may feel "cold" in another.

Sonic branding must respect—and reflect—the cultural landscape it lives in.

C. Psychographics – What Do They Believe In?

What are your audience's aspirations? Are they dreamers? Doers? Seekers of comfort or adventure?

For nature lovers, use earthy, organic tones. For fitness freaks, add beats and pace. For spiritual seekers, try ambient textures, bells, or chants. The more aligned your sound is with their values and lifestyle, the deeper the emotional bond.

Step 3: Composition – Stitching the Sonic Fabric

It's time to compose once you know who you are and who you're speaking to. This is where the art and science merge.

You start blending:
- Timbre (the character of the sound),
- Tempo (speed and energy),
- Tonality (major, minor, neutral),
- Instrumentation (digital vs acoustic, Indian vs Western),
- Texture (rich layering or minimal vibes).

It's like preparing a thali—every element must be balanced and harmonious. Too spicy, and it overwhelms. Too bland, and it forgets. The final piece should feel like it belongs. Like it's always been yours.

Step 4: Testing – The Soundcheck

It's not logical to just fall in love with your creation. Testing is the most vital step in your marketing journey.

How do people respond to it? Do they associate it with the right emotions? Is it memorable after one hearing? Does it work across TV, mobile, retail stores, radio, and digital platforms?

Sound behaves differently depending on context. What sounds heavenly in your designer headphones might fall flat on a cheap phone speaker. So, make it a point to test across touchpoints.

Most importantly, check emotional resonance. People don't always remember what they hear, but they *always* remember how it made them feel. In the later chapters, we reveal how neuroscience-based testing is now available to you to test your sonic branding and truly understand how consumers will feel when they hear it. It is truly pathbreaking.

Step 5: Consistency – The Long Play

Here's where most brands falter. They craft a beautiful sonic identity... and then change it every few months. But here's the thing: for sonic branding to work, consistency is needed. Use the same sound across your app, website, YouTube ads, customer service hold music, and, if possible, packaging experiences. Let that tune become *familiar*. Let it build *trust*. Think of it like your brand's fragrance. If it changes every time you meet someone, how will they ever recognize you?

Final Note: Sound is More Than Marketing

Crafting a sonic identity isn't just a marketing tactic. It's a commitment to being felt, not just seen.

Because when visuals fade and words are forgotten, *sound stays*. A little melody, a warm tone, a familiar hum—it can remind someone of who you are, what you mean, and why they care. So take your time.

Listen deeply. Compose with care. Your sound could be the most beautiful thing your brand ever says.

PART 3:
VISUAL INFLUENCE
The Brain's Obsession with Sight

6

WHY VISION IS THE BRAIN'S FAVORITE SENSE

Let me ask you something—if you had to give up one of your senses, which one would you fight the hardest to keep? For most of us, the answer is obvious: VISION. That's not surprising. Vision isn't just about looking at pretty sunsets or reading memes. It's the primary sense through which we interact with the world. And guess what? Our brains are *obsessed* with it. Nearly half of the human brain is directly or indirectly involved in visual processing. Think about that—half your brain's real estate is dedicated to seeing, interpreting, and reacting to your surroundings.

Why such an obsession? For humans, vision equals survival.

Back in the Stone Age, survival depended on spotting a predator lurking in the bushes or identifying which fruit was safe to eat. Even today, vision protects us—whether dodging a fast-approaching car or recognizing the "Wet Floor" sign before slipping.

Your eyes are constantly scanning for danger. And this isn't just about *seeing*—it's about interpreting visual cues quickly enough to respond. It's why our reaction times are often faster when we see a threat than when we hear or feel one. The same mechanism that helped our ancestors avoid saber-toothed tigers is now helping you avoid stepping on a Lego barefoot and avoid the pain it causes.

Seeing Is Connecting – Vision Builds Social Bonds

Now let's shift gears—vision isn't just about "fight or flight." It's also the glue of human connection.

Have you ever been in a room where someone's just raised their eyebrow, and you *knew* what they meant? Or smiled at a stranger and received a smile back? That's non-verbal communication, and it's all visual.

From reading facial expressions to decoding body language, vision allows us to connect, collaborate, and belong. In ancient tribes, being able to recognize group members—or detect deception from someone's eyes—meant safety. Today, the same instinct helps us bond during conversations, detect sarcasm, or sense tension in a meeting room.

Vision = Learning = Culture

Before language, before writing, there were pictures.

Cave paintings. Hand gestures. Symbols. These were our first tools for transferring knowledge. And what made it possible? Visual memory.

From ancient Egyptian hieroglyphics to modern infographics on Instagram, vision has always played a pivotal role in how we convey ideas. Our entire learning system is visual at its core—books, blackboards, presentations, even emojis.

Even deeper? Vision helps us read the environment. We notice that when the sky darkens, it signals rain. We scan for food, danger, or clues about what's coming next.

Basically, vision taught us how to interpret the world—and eventually, to shape it.

7

HOW THE BRAIN STORES WHAT WE SEE: VISUAL MEMORY

But Wait—Where Does "Seeing" Actually Happen? Here's a fun twist: most people think vision happens in the eyes. Not quite. The eyes are just the camera.

The brain is the studio, doing all the editing, color grading, and special effects. You can close your eyes and still "see" a mental image, right?

Or dream vividly while sleeping? That's because vision is not just about collecting light—it's about interpreting meaning. And that happens deep inside your brain.

So let's take a quick tour of how your brain processes vision.

Step-by-Step: The Brain's Visual Highway

  1. Light Enters the Eye: Light enters through the cornea, passes through the pupil, and is focused by the lens onto the retina. This is where things get technical—but fascinating.

The retina has two kinds of photoreceptors:
- Rods (night vision, shapes, motion)
- Cones (color, fine detail, daylight)

2. Light Becomes Electricity: Light stimulates a chemical reaction in the rods and cones, which converts light into electrical signals.

3. Signals Take the Highway: The optic nerve carries these signals to the brain. But something clever happens on the way—the optic nerves cross paths at the optic chiasm, helping the brain stitch together one cohesive image from both eyes.

4. First Pit Stop (LGN): The signals reach the thalamus's Lateral Geniculate Nucleus (LGN). This nucleus acts like a router, organizing and forwarding signals for deeper processing.

5. Visual Cortex (V1): The Brain's Graphics Card In the occipital lobe, the brain breaks things down further—edges, motion, orientation. Specialized neurons fire up to analyze what you're seeing.

6. Two Big Questions: What and Where?
- Dorsal stream ("Where is it?") → Helps track movement and position
- Ventral stream ("What is it?") → Helps identify objects, colors, faces

7. Integration: Your brain combines this visual information with touch, sound, smell, and even memories to create a 3D, sensory-rich understanding of your surroundings.

8. Action or Memory: The final decision: act on it, or store it. The prefrontal cortex might plan a response. The hippocampus might save it as a memory.

Either way, vision becomes part of how you think, feel, and behave. So yes, "seeing" is not just about detecting light. It's about interpreting, responding, and remembering what that light means. Now that we know how the brain processes images, let's explore how it stores them. In the modern, screen-satiated world that we live in, your brain is bombarded with thousands of visual inputs every day.

Street signs. Social media posts. Product packaging. People's faces. And yet...you don't remember all of it, right? That's because the brain is smart. It uses different types of memory to decide what's worth holding onto—and for how long.

Let's break it down.

- *Iconic Memory – The Blink-and-Gone Buffer*

Imagine a sparkler flashing for a split second in the dark. That fleeting trace? That's an iconic memory.

It lasts about 250 milliseconds—just enough time for the brain to decide: *"Should I keep this or toss it?"*

It's critical for smooth visual experiences. Think about reading a book or watching a video. You don't see each word or frame as separate—it all flows. That's thanks to iconic memory.

In marketing, this is why instant impact visuals matter. You only get a quarter of a second to catch someone's eye. That's why:

- Logos are bold
- Ads are flashy
- Visuals are simplified for immediate recognition

It's like love at first sight. You only have milliseconds to make a memory.

- *Visual Short-Term Memory (VSTM) – The Mental Clipboard*

Once something passes the Iconic memory filter, it may get stored in VSTM, like a scratchpad that holds visuals for a few seconds or minutes.

Some instances of this happening are when you are:

- Comparing two outfits
- Holding a phone number in your mind briefly
- Spotting a product on a shelf and remembering it as you browse

Most people can hold about 4 to 7 visual items in VSTM. And this memory fades fast unless repeated or reinforced.

Marketers apply this by:

- Using flash sales

- Showing eye-catching banners or pop-ups
- Creating special product displays on the shelves or Gondola ends The idea is simple: hold the image just long enough for a decision to be made.
- ***Visual Long-Term Memory (VLTM) – The Vault***

This is where iconic brands live. Coca-Cola red. Apple's bitten apple. Your childhood bedroom.

VLTM stores visual information for hours, years, even a lifetime, and there's no real limit to its capacity.

The catch? Only *emotionally relevant*, repeated, or meaningful visuals make it in.

Marketers build VLTM by:
- Using consistent logos and colors
- Telling emotional stories in their ads
- Creating distinctive packaging
- Associating visuals with positive experiences

That's why even 20 years later, you might remember a jingle or a billboard from your childhood. The brain tucked it away—probably because it made you feel something.

How Marketers Tap Into Our Visual Memory Systems

Suppose you've ever remembered a brand just by catching a quick flash of its logo or recalled an ad days after seeing it once.

Congrats, your brain is doing exactly what marketers hoped it would. In branding and advertising, visual memory isn't just a nice-to-have—it's the secret sauce.

Let's see how each memory type plays its part.

Iconic Memory in Marketing – Blink and Brand It

Here's the deal—iconic memory lasts less than a second, but that's more than enough time for a strong visual to sink in.

Think of it like this: You're scrolling Instagram or passing a billboard in a cab. You don't have time to "process" anything. But if done right, one colour, one shape, one image can stick.

That's why:
- Logos are made to be simple, bold, and instantly recognizable. Think: the Nike swoosh.
  You could spot it from across a field.
- Product packaging is designed to pop off shelves. A bright yellow chips packet? Your hand goes straight to it—even when your logical brain hasn't caught up yet.
- Flashy ads with moving visuals or high contrast make sure that even if you don't *consciously* read them, your subconscious stores a snapshot.

Ever notice how promotional displays in retail stores are shaped like oversized versions of products? A giant ketchup bottle? That's for iconic memory. It makes a quick impression and sparks recall the next time you're in that aisle.

Digital twist: Platforms like Instagram, TikTok, and Snapchat use this to the max—short, punchy visuals, optimized to register even if you scroll past in half a second.

- ***Visual Short-Term Memory (VSTM) – Holding On Just Long Enough***

Now, suppose you see an online ad for a new chocolate bar. You don't buy it right away. But a few minutes later, you're near a shop—and boom! You spot the same bar, and your brain says: "Aha! Try that one!"

That's VSTM doing its job. It held that the visual image just long enough for you to act on it.

Marketers love VSTM for:
- **Flash sales or countdown timers:** They grab your attention and demand quick action. "Only 2 hours left!"—and suddenly, you remember that banner long enough to click.
- **Pop-up ads:** These are designed to stay in your mind for a few minutes, even after you've dismissed them.
- **Interactive content:** Memory games, short quizzes, or "Tap to Reveal" elements often require you to remember something for 10–30 seconds, just long

enough to build engagement.
- **Product tutorials:** Quick video demos that show *how to use* something give just enough time for the key visuals to imprint on your short-term memory.
- **In-store example:** Point-of-sale (POS) displays are designed to hit VSTM. Bright colors, limited-time offers, and emotional imagery make you stop, look, and (hopefully) buy.
- **Email campaigns:** The subject line with emojis, bold headers, and countdown clocks—these use VSTM to keep the offer top-of-mind long enough for action.

- *Visual Long-Term Memory (VLTM) – Where Brands Live Forever*

This is the big league. VLTM is what ensures you remember that "Dairy Milk = Comfort", or that your childhood birthday cake had Britannia written in white and red icing.

VLTM is where brands build loyalty.

To enter this memory bank, visuals must be:
- Emotional – they need to make you feel something.
- Repetitive – the more you see it, the deeper it's stored.
- Distinctive – if it's generic, the brain tosses it out.

Here's how marketers work their magic:

1. Consistency Across Time

Brands that use the same colors, fonts, and logos across all platforms—TV, print, digital, packaging—tend to be remembered longer. Example: Coca-Cola's red & white theme hasn't changed in over a century. No wonder it's hard-wired into global memory.

2. Emotional Storytelling

Think of those heartwarming Christmas ads or nostalgia-led campaigns that bring tears (or at least a smile). These ads aim for emotional encoding, where the brain associates a brand with a specific feeling. The reason emotional ads work better is rooted in neuroscience. The amygdala[3], the brain's emotion processor, works closely with the hippocampus, which handles memory storage.

When something triggers an emotional reaction—especially joy, surprise, or nostalgia—it boosts memory consolidation. So a cute dog in a commercial isn't just to melt hearts—it's a strategic way to make the ad unforgettable.

Example: John Lewis Christmas ads in the UK, or the classic Amul billboard series in India with witty, emotional appeal—these aren't just ads. They're mini memories.

3. Celebrity Endorsements

When you see a familiar face like Shah Rukh Khan or Virat Kohli associated with a brand, your long-term memory lights up. That's because faces are sticky in our brain's memory system. We store faces more efficiently than abstract images.

4. Unique Packaging

Ever noticed how you can spot a Parle-G biscuit packet in a crowd? That beige pack with the girl on it hasn't changed in decades. It's not just packaging—it's a nostalgia portal.

5. Iconic Campaigns & Slogans

Some lines stay in our heads forever:
- "Just Do It." (Nike)
- "I'm Lovin' It." (McDonald's)
- "Thanda Matlab Coca-Cola." (India-specific, but timeless)

These are tied to visuals and jingles that keep resurfacing every time you see or hear them again. That's long-term branding magic.

Marketers don't just design for aesthetics—they design for memory.

- Iconic memory → Blink-fast recognition (logos, colour flashes, bold packaging)
- VSTM → Short-term nudges (timed offers, demos, pop-ups)
- VLTM → Brand identity and loyalty (emotions, stories, repetition) And when all three work together? That's how an ordinary ad turns into a lifelong consumer relationship.

8

VISUAL ELEMENTS THAT STICK

Imagine you're walking through a supermarket aisle, completely distracted by your phone. Suddenly, something bright and red catches your eye.

You glance up, and without thinking, you reach for that familiar cola bottle. You didn't plan it. You didn't even consciously choose it. But your brain did. That's the power of visual elements in marketing. They don't shout; they *whisper straight to the subconscious.*

Colour, shape, logos, even fonts—they quietly guide your behavior. In fact, most of the time, they do this without asking for permission. Welcome to the world of neuromarketing, where visual design speaks directly to your neural circuits.

Let's unpack how each of these visual elements affects the brain and why brands spend millions obsessing over them.

COLOR – Not Just a Visual Treat, but a Neuro-Hack

You might think colour is just about aesthetics. Something that makes packaging "look nice."

But ask any good marketer—or better yet, a neuroscientist—and they'll tell you: colour is emotional currency.

Why do fast food joints like McDonald's, KFC, and Burger King all use red and yellow? It's not a coincidence. Red triggers appetite, speeds up your pulse, and conveys urgency. Yellow, on the other hand, evokes warmth, cheerfulness, and hunger. Put them together and you've got the perfect cocktail to lure you into a quick meal.

Let's try a quick experiment—close your eyes and picture the following:

- A blue bank logo—safe and dependable, right?
- A green juice bottle—seems healthy already, doesn't it?
- A black perfume ad—ah, that feels premium, maybe even seductive.

You didn't see any text or hear any voiceover, but still, you formed a story in your mind. That's the brain's response to colour association, a concept rooted in both psychology and neurobiology.

Even cultural context plays a role. In Western cultures, white means purity. In some Asian cultures, it's associated with mourning. This makes global branding a high-stakes game—because your red in China may not say the same thing in Sweden.

And did you know that using the right colors on a website or product page can directly impact conversion rates? A subtle switch from green to orange for a "Buy Now" button has boosted clicks for many brands. Colour speaks to the lizard brain—the primitive part of us that acts before we think.

SHAPES – The Brain's Silent Storytellers

We might not think much about shapes, but our brains do. Shapes are like the *body language* of design.

Even before you read a word or see a colour, the logo or package shape gives you a gut feeling. That's because the brain is wired to find meaning in visual form.

Let's walk through a few examples:
- **Circles and curves:** Have you noticed how baby products or community-driven brands often use round logos? Circles feel soft, safe, and welcoming.
  Brands like Pepsi or Airbnb leverage this to signal friendliness.
- **Squares and rectangles:** These feel grounded and secure. There's a sense of structure and order here, which is why you'll find companies like IBM and Microsoft sticking to boxy shapes. They tell you, "We're stable, you can trust us."
- **Triangles:** Now this one's interesting. Triangles, especially when pointed upwards, scream ambition, power, and direction. Tech and finance brands often use this to imply growth or innovation—think Adidas or even the Delta Airlines logo.

Even a shape's orientation matters. A triangle pointing up feels strong. Pointing down feels unstable or aggressive. Now think about packaging. Ever held a perfume bottle shaped like a sleek curve? You likely felt it was more "luxurious" than one in a standard rectangular bottle, right? That's no accident. The way something feels in your hand—even if you're not thinking about it—tells your brain a story.

ANTHROPOMORPHISM & MASCOTS – When Brands Wear a Face

Let's say you're at a theme park, and your kid runs up to hug a life-sized M&M's character. What just happened?

That's anthropomorphism in action—the human tendency to give non-human things human traits. And in marketing, it's absolute gold.

Brands have long known this trick. You slap a pair of eyes and a big smile on something—suddenly, people trust it more.

Take Tony the Tiger—he's not just selling cereal, he's saying, "Hey kid, let's have a grrreat morning together!" That connection? That's emotional branding. And trust me, the brain *loves* it.

Or think about Mr. Clean—a muscular guy with a spotless white shirt and an earring. That's not just a cleaner—it's a *personality*. The product now feels like someone who can rescue your kitchen from chaos.

Even insurance companies—a boring space by all means—use this trick. The Geico Gecko adds humor and charm to what would otherwise be a dry product. And it works! Studies using EEG and eye-tracking show that we remember mascots more easily than static logos.

It's like our brains say: "If it looks like a friend, talks like a friend, must be a friend."

LOGOS – Your Visual Signature

Now, imagine the Apple logo without the bite. Would it feel the same?

Logos are so much more than artistic symbols. They're cognitive shortcuts. The brain loves familiarity, and a logo, if done well, becomes the face of that comfort.

Take the Nike Swoosh. It's barely a shape. But it *feels* like motion. Like progress. Like energy. It doesn't need words. One glance, and your brain says: "I know this. I trust this."

Neuromarketing research shows that the most effective logos are:
- Simple – Easy to store and recall.
- Distinct – Unique enough to stand out.
- Emotionally linked – Either through colour, shape, or memory.

And if you think it's just about attention, you'd be mistaken. A good logo influences trust, decision-making, and even perceived product value.

Ever noticed how luxury brands often use clean, bold logos with lots of white space? That's no accident. **Simplicity = confidence = premium perception.**

TYPOGRAPHY – When Fonts Speak Louder Than Words

You may not remember what an ad said, but if the font was ugly or hard to read, you definitely noticed.

Fonts carry personality. Just like colour and shape, your brain reads typography emotionally. The font used by a law firm is going to be very different from the one used by a boutique cupcake brand, and rightly so.

Let's decode:

- Serif fonts – Traditional, reliable. Great for newspapers, universities, and legacy brands.
- Sans-serif fonts – Clean, modern, neutral. Ideal for tech companies and startups.
- Script fonts – Elegant, emotional. Best used sparingly, often for luxury or feminine products.
- Bold display fonts – Loud and proud. Used when you want to *shout* an offer or create urgency.

Typography also affects readability, which affects cognitive load. If your brain has to work hard to decipher your message, it's less likely to remember it. That's why smart brands go for clean, well-spaced fonts that flow easily across platforms.

Amazon's typography? Simple and consistent. And that consistency builds trust. It says, "We know who we are."

Visual elements are not there just to "make things pretty." They're powerful tools that interface directly with your brain's emotional and memory systems. Colour triggers feelings, shapes whisper meaning, mascots create relationships, logos build identity, and fonts... fonts speak your brand's inner voice.

And the best part? All this happens *below* the level of conscious awareness.

As a marketer, designer, or business owner, knowing how to wield these tools responsibly and creatively is like holding the keys to the consumer's mind.

So next time you scroll past an ad and feel a strange pull, just know, it's not magic. It's neuroscience.

PART 4:
THE POWER OF TOUCH
The Forgotten Sense That Shapes Brand Perception

9

HOW HAPTIC MEMORY WORKS

Let me tell you about a rather clever experiment a luxury car brand once ran. Picture this: two sleek, shiny cars parked side by side in a posh showroom. On the surface, they looked the same—same model, color, and everything. The catch? One had your standard plastic interiors, the kind that feel a bit cold and lifeless. The other? Lush, buttery leather that almost hugged your fingers.

Now, here's where it gets interesting. The guests who came in had no clue about the difference. They sat inside both cars, ran their fingers across the surfaces, maybe even imagined themselves cruising down the highway. Later, when asked which one felt more luxurious or reliable, the overwhelming majority picked the leather-finished car. Same specs, same engine. Just a different texture. Crazy, right?

That, my friend, is the power of haptic memory—our ability to remember and emotionally respond to things we've touched. It's not just about recognizing a texture. It's about the feelings that texture triggers. Softness often signals luxury. Roughness might imply ruggedness or even discomfort. And these associations, once built, can be powerful brand cues.

In today's hyper-visual world, where every brand is shouting for attention with flashy graphics and snappy videos, the ones that manage to engage your sense of touch? They stand out. It's like walking into a store and touching a cashmere scarf — your fingers *just know* it's special. You remember how it felt, long after the image fades. Now, here's the science-y bit: it's fascinating.

Haptic memory can be short-term or long-term. The long-term stuff sticks because either the touch was repeated (like playing the same piano piece a hundred times) or because it was significant enough to get etched into your brain. Ever reach into your pocket and instantly tell a coin from a key? That's long-term haptic memory doing its job — no eyes needed.

And here's the fun part for marketers: Haptic memory isn't just a survival mechanism. It's a subtle tool to create brand loyalty. Think about unboxing a new iPhone. The gentle pull of the lid, the cold metal edges, the satisfying click of the buttons — it's not by accident. Apple's practically telling your fingers, "This is what premium feels like." And guess what? Your fingers remember.

Haptics Processing and the Somatosensory Cortex

So, how exactly does your brain know the difference between silk and sandpaper? Or why your fingers can feel the tiniest bump, while your back might barely register a mosquito bite? The answer lies deep inside your brain, in the somatosensory cortex.

Now, don't let the big term scare you. Think of the somatosensory cortex as your brain's very own touch translator — it takes the raw signals from your skin, muscles, and joints, and turns them into meaning. Whether a needle's prick or a feather's soft brush, this part of the brain figures out what's touching you, how hard, where, and what it means. Technically, this cortex is split into smaller zones. There's Area 3a, which deals with movement feedback from your muscles and joints. Then there's Area 3b, which gets direct input from your skin — your texture radar. Area 1 dives into fine details like smoothness or grit, while Area 2 handles more abstract stuff like the shape and size of things you touch.

But it gets cooler. The brain doesn't treat all parts of your body equally. Enter the sensory homunculus — a wildly disproportionate little brain map that looks like a strange cartoon figure. In this map, the size of each body part is based not on how big it is in real life, but how sensitive it is to touch. That's why your hands, lips, and face occupy the most space — they're packed with touch receptors and constantly feed your brain with rich sensory info. Imagine a sculptor's hands, moving instinctively over clay. Or a child testing food with their lips before taking a bite. Thanks to this beautifully detailed wiring system, those body parts send non-stop updates to the brain. Now, the journey of a touch signal is like a relay race. Tiny receptors under your skin convert that physical sensation into an electrical impulse when you touch something. This impulse zips through your nerves, travels up the spinal cord, takes a pitstop at the medulla oblongata, and then checks in with the thalamus, which acts like a sensory gatekeeper. Finally, the signal lands in the primary somatosensory cortex (S1), where it gets fully processed.

And here's the kicker: your brain doesn't just process these touch signals in isolation. It cross-talks with other parts, like the visual and auditory centers, so your touch perception can link up with what you see or hear.

That's how you can look at a wool sweater, touch it, and immediately get a sense of how cozy (or itchy) it might feel. This integration gives us that magical, all-sensory awareness of our world—and it's gold for marketers who want to make lasting impressions.

Understanding the Sensory Homunculus

Let's return to that funky brain map I mentioned: the sensory homunculus. If you've never seen it, do yourself a favor and look it up sometime. It's this weird, distorted human figure with enormous lips and hands, exaggerated tongue and face, and hilariously tiny legs.

It's not just some artistic exaggeration — it actually reflects how much brainpower is dedicated to processing touch from each body part.

Your fingertips, for example, are off-the-charts sensitive. They're loaded with mechanoreceptors, especially little guys called Merkel cells and Meissner's corpuscles, which help detect even the softest brush or tiniest bump. That's why you can read Braille with your fingers or feel the raised lettering on a credit card. And guess what? A big chunk of your somatosensory cortex is just sitting there, devoted to interpreting what your fingers are up to. The lips are another hotspot — and it's no coincidence we use them for eating, speaking, and...kissing. All of these involve subtle, rich sensory feedback. That's why a quick brush on the lips can trigger a cascade of emotional and physical responses.

The face — especially around the cheeks, mouth, and forehead — is packed with touch sensors too. It's how we pick up on social cues. A tiny change in temperature or pressure can tell us a lot — whether someone's blushing, frowning, or leaning in for a hug.

The tongue, now that's a multitasker. It doesn't just detect taste — it feels texture too. Is that chocolate smooth or gritty? Is the food hot or icy cold? Even while we're talking, the tongue constantly feels our words' shape. It's like a sensory ninja. Feet are unsung heroes. Covered in pressure and vibration sensors, they help us stay upright, adjust our gait, and detect terrain. Thanks to those brilliant sensors, you'll walk barefoot on pebbles, and you'll feel every tiny shift. And yes, we can't leave out the genitals, especially the clitoris and penis, which are among the most sensitive areas of the body — not just biologically, but emotionally too.

Their sensitivity plays a big role in intimacy and bonding. It's deeply human. Even the ears and neck have high touch sensitivity — think goosebumps when someone whispers too close, or the gentle shiver from a cool breeze. These regions are subtle communicators in both social and intimate settings. From a neuromarketing perspective, understanding this sensory real estate is priceless. If you want people to remember your brand—not just see it but feel it—focus on the fingers, the lips, the face, and the tongue. These are the gateways to emotional, tactile memory.

10

NEUROMARKETING APPLICATIONS OF TOUCH

Okay, now that we've taken a little tour of how touch works in the brain, let's bring it back to the marketing world.

Because, honestly, what good is all that brain science if we can't apply it to the art of winning hearts and wallets?

In the realm of neuromarketing, touch is a game-changer. Why? Because it's one of our most emotionally potent and memory-triggering senses. You can forget what something looked like, but not the feel of it. That sticks.

Think about the last time you opened a new gadget or peeled the lid off a fancy ice cream tub. Wasn't it satisfying?

Let's break this down into three major ways touch is leveraged in marketing:

- Product feel
- Texture and in-mouth sensory
- Packaging and in-store tactile experiences

Product Feel – When Touch Sells

Let's talk about Apple. (You probably knew that was coming, right?)

There's a reason why people rave not just about how an iPhone *works*, but how it *feels*. The smooth coolness of the aluminum, the weight of it in your palm, the satisfying click of the buttons — it's all designed, engineered, and obsessively tested. Even the unboxing experience is choreographed like a luxury ritual. That slow, almost poetic release of the box lid? Yeah, that's no accident. It's built to make you feel like you're opening a treasure, not just a phone.

That tactile luxury tells your brain, "This is quality." And the brain listens.

Now, swing over to Lush Cosmetics. Walk into one of their stores and you're encouraged—no, *invited*—to touch everything. The creamy lotions, the fizzy bath bombs, the grainy scrubs. It's like a candy store for your hands. And what's more human than using touch to explore and make sense of the world? This hands-on approach doesn't just lead to purchases—it creates little memory anchors. "Oh yeah, I loved how that face mask felt." Boom. Connection made.

Even humble old KitKat gets this right. The iconic snap when you break a finger off? It's like striking the proverbial tactile gold. There's something oddly satisfying about that crisp break, like your fingers are part of the ritual. Pair that with the line "Have a break, have a KitKat," and you've got a perfect storm of physical sensation, memory, and emotional branding.

Texture – The Unsung Hero of Taste

Alright, let's step into your mouth for a second (that sounded less weird in my head, I promise).

When it comes to food and drinks, we often forget that *texture* is a *huge* part of the experience. Think about it: creamy equals comforting. Crunchy feels exciting.

Velvety? Luxurious. Gritty? Hmm... maybe a bit rustic or unrefined.

Our brains are wired to interpret these textures as emotional signals. That's why your brain gets a tiny dopamine hit when you bite into a crispy chip or swirl a silky hot chocolate around your tongue. It's not just about taste, it's about mouthfeel.

Brands get this. Chocolate companies like Lindt know their way around a melt-in-the-mouth moment. Their ads often focus on how the chocolate dissolves — smooth, slow, sensual. On the flip side, brands like Lay's hype up the crunch, the crackle, the *sound* of biting in, because that equals fun and satisfaction.

Even beverages play the texture game. Think of that creamy froth on a cappuccino or the sharp fizz of a cola hitting the back of your throat. These tactile signatures stick in your memory and in your buying decisions.

Packaging – Haptic Memory's Trojan Horse

Now here's where it gets even more fascinating: packaging. It's not just a container — it's a sensory experience waiting to happen.

Take Danone's Aqua in Indonesia. They redesigned their bottle with mountain-shaped ridges. Why? To subconsciously associate the product with pure, natural mountain water. That design stuck—literally and mentally. Consumers didn't just see the difference; they felt it, and that feeling became part of the brand's story.

Häagen-Dazs went a step further. Their ice cream tubs use a unique, soft-touch lid — it almost feels velvety. It's a small detail, but it creates an emotional moment. You feel like you're treating yourself to something luxurious before the spoon even hits your tongue. And who could forget Toblerone? The iconic triangle-shaped packaging isn't just about looking different on the shelf — it makes you *engage* with it. Snapping off those chocolate peaks becomes part of the experience. That, my friend, is haptic memory in action. Even Febreze figured this out. Their redesigned spray bottles now have an ergonomic grip and a smooth, satisfying trigger pull. That pleasant hand-feel makes you think, "This product works well," even before you smell a thing. That's the psychology of touch influencing the perception of function.

In-Store Experiences

Now, what about retail spaces? Can you design a physical environment to trigger haptic memory and emotional bonding? Absolutely. Just ask Apple (again.) Their stores are temples of tactile luxury.

The moment you walk in, you're encouraged to touch, swipe, tap, and feel. You don't just see the MacBook; everyone in that store is gently pressing the keys, dragging their hands across the top cover to see how sleek it feels, even scrutinizing the display. Everyone is concerned about the feel of it.

Over at IKEA, it's the same logic. They don't just show you a couch, they let you sit on it, lounge a little, feel the texture of the cushions, and open the drawers in the mock kitchen. It's not window shopping — it's interactive storytelling. You start imagining their furniture in *your* home, wondering which side of the room it will look best in, and whether the curtains will clash with the couch. That physical interaction starts shaping your decision-making. Sephora? Another touch genius. Testers everywhere. You can swipe on lipsticks, dab on creams, and even smell perfumes. The result? You get attached to the product before you've even bought it. You've already touched it. It's yours, emotionally. Nike does it too — from trial treadmills to customizing sneakers with your own hands. They turn retail into a playground, one where your body and your brain both get involved.

Wrapping It Up (with Texture, of Course)

Touch isn't just a supporting actor in the marketing mix — it's a leading star that too often gets overlooked. But now, with all we know about haptic memory, tactile processing, and somatosensory mapping, it's time to give it center stage. Touch can create emotional stickiness, whether it's the cold aluminum of a MacBook, the sandy crunch of a Lush scrub, or the soft pull of a chocolate bar wrapper. And when a brand taps into that... well, let's say your fingers will remember long after your eyes forget.

PART 5:
SMELL AND TASTE SYNERGY
Creating Brands That Are Craved For

11

HOW SMELL AND TASTE WORK

Let me start with a story. Imagine an ordinary day in Indonesia. You're casually strolling past a little shop, a warung, not hungry, with no plans of eating anything. But suddenly your eyes land on that brightly colored packet—yes, it's Indomie Mi Goreng. Immediately, your mouth waters, and your brain starts recalling how delicious those noodles taste. Strange, isn't it? You weren't even hungry! That's because your brain has developed something called sensory memory, linking sight with taste & flavor.

This kind of sensory memory is what brands crave—it turns the packaging itself into a silent salesperson. Just seeing it can trigger desire, even without hunger.

Olfactory and Gustatory Sense: The Science Behind the Magic

Before diving deeper, it's crucial to grasp how our senses of smell (olfaction) and taste (gustation) work together to shape our food experiences. Ever eaten something so bad you couldn't even look at it again? Blame your sensory memory for that.

Let's get technical but simple. Smell works like this: when you breathe, odor molecules float into your nose and stick onto tiny olfactory receptors inside your nasal cavity. Humans have around 400 different types of these receptors, each sensitive to specific scents. Once activated, these receptors send signals to your olfactory bulb, a part of your brain right above the nasal cavity. Here, signals are grouped and processed, then passed to the olfactory cortex in the temporal lobe. Interestingly, this area directly connects to the amygdala[3] (the emotional hub) and hippocampus (your brain's memory center). That explains why certain smells take you back to grandma's kitchen or childhood.

Taste is slightly simpler but equally fascinating. Your tongue and throat have taste buds with gustatory cells, detecting the five basic tastes: sweet, sour, salty, bitter, and umami (savory). These cells send signals through three cranial nerves, converging in a part of your brainstem called the nucleus of the solitary tract. Then, signals travel to your thalamus (the brain's main relay center) and finally reach the primary gustatory cortex in your insula and frontal operculum. And voila, you experience taste.

Together, smell and taste create a symphony called "flavor." Try pinching your nose while eating; you'll quickly realize how dull food tastes without smell. Ever wondered why bitter medicines seem less horrible when you block your nose? Now you know.

Why Smell Wins the Sensory Battle

Believe it or not, smell plays a far greater role than taste. Here's why:

1. Wide Range of Detection: Your nose can distinguish thousands of smells—fresh bread, roses, wet soil after rain—but your tongue has just five basic tastes. The wide variety of aromas humans detect is brilliantly represented by something called Aroma Wheels.

2. Flavor Perception: About 80% of flavor perception depends on smell. That's why food tastes bland when you have a cold. No smell equals no flavor.

3. Emotional and Memory Bonds: Your sense of smell directly links to your emotional and memory centers. Remember our Indomie story? Just the smell of it cooking evokes strong emotions and powerful memories, leading to instant cravings.

4. Safety and Survival: Smell alerts us to dangers, from smoke to spoiled food. Imagine smelling gas before a leak becomes dangerous—pretty lifesaving, right?

- **Appetite Influence:** Smells can stimulate hunger or suppress appetite. Think freshly baked bread versus rotten garbage. One boosts your appetite, the other destroys it completely.
- **Nonverbal Communication:** Have you ever heard of pheromones? These subtle chemicals affect human attraction and bonding without us consciously realizing it.
- Clearly, smell isn't just important—it's essential. It's the spice of life, giving depth and color to our experiences.

12

LEVERAGING OLFACTORY & GUSTATORY MEMORY IN MARKETING

Olfactory memory can be strategically used at every marketing stage, from product development to post-purchase engagement. Let's explore this further.

Product Development
Why Certain Flavors Rule & New Flavors Often Flop

Flavor acceptance can make or break products. But why do some flavors dominate sales charts while new flavors often fail miserably?

The secret is neuroscience. Our brains love familiar tastes because they activate the reward system—specifically, dopamine release, a neurotransmitter tied to pleasure and reinforcement. Familiar tastes trigger oxytocin, a hormone linked to bonding and satisfaction, making us crave them repeatedly.

Additionally, flavors tied to happy childhood memories can deeply imprint themselves in our brains via the hippocampus and amygdala[3], creating strong emotional ties and brand loyalty.

Consumers might claim they love new flavors, but their shopping behavior usually disagrees. New flavors often lack the emotional and memory-driven responses associated with familiar ones.

Without oxytocin-triggered cravings, new tastes struggle to attract buyers.

So, how can marketers overcome this?

- **Bridge Flavors:** Introduce new flavors slowly by mixing them with familiar tastes.
- **Limited Editions:** These create urgency and exclusivity, enticing consumers to experiment.
- **Sampling:** Giving consumers firsthand experiences boosts familiarity and purchase likelihood.
- **Emotional Marketing:** Connecting flavors to emotions through storytelling or influencer testimonials makes new flavors more relatable.

Advertisement Development

Because smell is directly wired to the brain's memory and emotion centers, even just *suggesting* a familiar scent in an ad, like fresh coffee or rain on dry earth, can instantly trigger powerful memories and feelings that make the brand more memorable and emotionally sticky.

Since we can't transmit smells through screens (yet), marketers rely on indirect methods to trigger olfactory memory. Here's how:

- **Evocative Imagery:** Vivid visuals, like steaming coffee, blooming flowers, prompt viewers to recall associated scents.
- **Descriptive Language:** Terms like "rich chocolate aroma" evoke sensory imagination.
- **Auditory Cues:** Sounds like coffee pouring or bread crust cracking reinforce imagined smells.
- **Celebrity Endorsements:** Authentic stories from celebrities about their sensory experiences enhance emotional connections.

Shopper Marketing

In shopper marketing, olfactory memory is a game-changer—just a whiff of a familiar scent, like fresh bread or baby powder, can subconsciously trigger comfort, nostalgia, or trust, nudging shoppers toward a spontaneous purchase without them even realizing why. Here's how to effectively use olfactory memory in retail:

- **Ambience:** Ambient scents aligned with store themes can dramatically boost customer experience. Think freshly baked bread in a bakery or soothing botanical scents in a natural cosmetics store.
- **Tester Packs:** Allowing consumers to experience fragrances directly boosts their confidence in purchasing. Sephora's extensive use of testers has successfully proven this method's effectiveness.

Essential Tips for Effective Olfactory Marketing

Consistency is key. Using the same scent across various touchpoints—stores, packaging, and promotions—reinforces brand recall. Also, ensure the fragrance aligns perfectly with your brand values.

Finally, sensory testing and consumer feedback refine scent strategies, helping brands tailor their scents effectively to consumer preferences.

In a nutshell, taste might be the front-runner when you eat, but smell is the secret ingredient enriching every experience and memory you create. Understanding and harnessing this powerful sense can significantly boost your brand's emotional connection with customers, ultimately driving greater loyalty and long-term success.

PART 6:
EXPERIENCE MEMORY

Creating Lasting Impressions

13

WHEN ALL YOUR MEMORIES COME TOGETHER

Let's start with something simple.

Ever walked into a room and suddenly felt like you'd time-travelled to a moment from years ago? Maybe it's the smell of jasmine flowers, or that old Bollywood song playing in the background, and — boom! You're right back at your cousin's wedding or a family Diwali night.

That's not magic. That's experiential memory.

In neuroscience, it's formally called episodic memory, a part of your long-term memory. But honestly, that sounds a bit too clinical, right? What it really is — is your brain's treasure chest of lived moments. These aren't just facts or dates. They're the moments that made you feel something. The kind of memories that still have colour, texture, smell... even warmth.

Think about it:
- The fresh, nervous excitement you felt on your first day of work, even how the air smelled that morning.

- The sound of your best friend laughing on a summer road trip echoes in your head like it was just yesterday.
- That flaky, buttery croissant you ate at a tiny café in Paris, and now, every time you have one, you're back there for a second.

This kind of memory doesn't work in isolation. It's layered. It's built on sight, sound, scent, taste, touch, all coming together like a beautifully woven saree. And it's usually sparked by the tiniest triggers—a sound, a smell, a particular texture.

Now, here's the interesting part — this isn't just personal. Brands want to live in that memory space, too. In fact, neuromarketing is all about figuring out how to place a brand experience in this emotional, sensory-heavy part of your brain. Why? Because when your brain remembers how something *felt*, your heart usually makes the decision.

Let's unpack this a little more.

- **Experience Memory Fuels Emotional Decisions**

Most of us like to believe we're logical creatures. But neuroscience says otherwise. We make the majority of our decisions *emotionally* and then justify them logically. It's like eating that chocolate cake and then later saying it was because of the antioxidants in dark chocolate.

So, when a brand manages to create an emotional memory — the joy of tasting a new snack at a friend's house, your brain stores it. Next time you see that same snack on the shelf, you don't consciously recall that memory, but your hand reaches out anyway. Why? Because your brain quietly nudged you, saying, "Remember how happy that made you feel?"

- **Sensory Cues Tap Into This Memory**

Brands that go beyond just visuals — that also use sound, touch, taste, even smell — get remembered better. That's why *sensory branding* is such a big deal in neuromarketing. It gives your memory more hooks to hang on to.

Ever walked into a store and instantly felt comforted just by the smell? That's deliberate.

Brands use these tiny sensory touches to stay in your memory. And once they're in, they're hard to shake.

- **Memory Creates Loyalty**

This part is simple. When you have a good experience, you remember it. And when a brand becomes part of that positive experience, you're more likely to stick with it, recommend it, even defend it in debates with friends (we've all done it!).

Good memories become good feelings. Good feelings become brand love.

So...How Does the Brain Store These Experience Memories?

Okay, let's geek out a bit — but don't worry, I'll keep it fun. Experience memory is stored through a beautifully orchestrated process involving various parts of your brain. It's not like one drawer where you keep everything. It's more like a massive storage unit, with different sections lit up based on what the memory involves.

Step 1:. Encoding: How Experience Becomes Memory

This is step one. Your brain takes in all the sights, sounds, and smells and starts filing them in the right places.

- **Sensory Cortex:** Each sense has its own processing center. Visuals go to the visual cortex. Sounds are to the auditory. Smells are to the olfactory. They don't just sit in isolation — they all connect to form one vivid, layered experience. That's why your memory of your grandmother's kitchen includes how it looked, the clinking of steel utensils, and the smell of fresh coriander.
- **Hippocampus:** This is the librarian of your memory system. It pulls together all the sensory info and adds emotional context. Initially, memories live here temporarily, but over time, they get passed on to long-term storage in the cortex — a process called memory consolidation.
- **Amygdala:** This one's the emotional DJ. It amplifies memories tied to strong emotions—especially fear, love, and pleasure. If something made your heart race or melt, the amygdala[3] ensures it's saved in HD.

Step 2: Retrieval: How You Revisit Those Memories

Now comes the magic trick — recalling a memory. It can feel effortless, but under the hood, your brain's doing some pretty intense gymnastics.

When something familiar happens—say, you hear a song from your school days or smell your mom's cooking—it's like someone tugging a thread. The brain starts pulling on that thread, and suddenly, all those scattered pieces light up. The emotion, the image, the smell, even the temperature of the day—it all rushes back. Your brain recalls memories by *reactivating the original network of senses, emotions, and context*, like replaying a scene from a movie you didn't even know you remembered. Essentially, there are three key components of Memory recall.

- **Cued Recall:** One small sensory input — like a familiar song or the smell of rain on dry soil — suddenly, an entire memory unrolls.
- **Hippocampal Reactivation:** The hippocampus gets reactivated and reawakens the sensory networks that stored the experience. It's like playing back a recording — except it's all happening inside your head.
- **Emotional Boost:** Thanks to the amygdala[3], memories with strong emotions are recalled faster and more vividly. That's why heartbreaks, victories, and childhood joys are so accessible.

What Makes a Memory Stick?

A few things tip the scales:

- **Emotional Intensity:** You remember things that made you *feel*. No one remembers every breakfast, but you'll never forget that one awkward job interview or that magical proposal under the stars. Emotions turn up the volume.
- **Frequency of Recall:** The more you remember something, the stronger it becomes. This is why embarrassing memories haunt us more than we'd like — we keep replaying them!

- **Context:** Sometimes, just being in the same place can help you remember.

That's why retracing your steps when you lose something actually works — it reactivates the context cues.

So yes, your brain is a master archivist — constantly recording, sorting, tagging, and re-playing experience memories based on how they made you feel and what senses were involved.

14

HOW EXPERIENCE MEMORY SHAPES THE 6PS OF MARKETING

Now that we understand how experience memory works, let's bring it home — how does this apply to marketing? Let's examine the 6Ps: Product, Price, Place, Promotion, People, and Process. Each one offers a golden opportunity to create *memorable* brand experiences.

1. Product Memory
A great product doesn't just solve a problem — it *feels* good.
- The texture of the packaging.
- The scent that hits you when you open it.
- The way it fits in your hand or melts in your mouth.

These tiny details—if done right—become sensory bookmarks. So next time the consumer sees your product, their brain says, "Oh yes, *this* one."

2. Price Memory
Price isn't just about numbers. It's about perception.
If your product has given a consumer a meaningful, positive

experience, they're more likely to associate the *price* with value, even if you're charging more than competitors. That's how brands move into the premium category, not just by pricing, but by experience. And once your brand gets labelled in someone's brain as "worth it," it's hard to dislodge.

3. Place Memory

Whether it's a fancy retail store or a clean, intuitive app, your brand's environment matters. Lighting, music, layout, and ease of navigation all contribute to the mood of the moment. If positive, that mood becomes a memory, one that gently pushes a consumer to come back.

4. Promotion Memory (Communications)

We've all seen ads that don't really "say" anything but leave us feeling something. That's the kind of promotion that uses experience memory smartly. An ad that makes you smile, cry, or feel proud — it's planting emotional seeds. And later, those seeds bloom into brand recall.

5. People Memory

Especially in the service industry, people are the face of the brand. A warm smile from the delivery guy or a helpful customer care executive — these interactions shape how we *feel* about a brand. And feeling, as we now know, is what the brain remembers best.

6. Process Memory

From clicking "Buy Now" to the package arriving at your door, the process matters. If it's smooth, quick, and enjoyable, that's a positive experience stored away. Suppose it's messy, confusing, or frustrating, that gets stored too. And guess which one encourages repeat purchase?

To Wrap It Up...

Experience memory is where brand loyalty is born. It's not in the ads, or the slogans, or the discounts. It's in the way a brand *makes someone feel*. And when that feeling is wrapped in sensory richness and emotional resonance, it becomes a memory. And memories — they don't just sit in our heads. They drive our hearts.

PART 7:
THE 6PS AND THE BRAIN
Rewiring Marketing Mix with Neuroscience

15

6PS OF MARKETING FROM A NEUROSCIENCE PERSPECTIVE

Alright, we briefly touched upon the 6Ps in the previous chapter, but now let's dig deeper into them — not the basic aspects which your business school textbooks drummed in, but the evolved, experience-driven version that makes sense in today's fast-moving, hyper-connected world.

Originally, there were only 4Ps: Product, Price, Place, Promotion. But in the service industries or highly emotional consumer categories, that's not quite enough anymore. Enter: People and Process, the extra layers that add depth, empathy, and stickiness to your strategy. These six dimensions don't just sell — they connect, linger, and build memory.

Let's examine each one with a fresh lens—one that links it to sensory memory and how people truly feel and remember brands.

Product

Let's start at the heart of the whole thing: your product. It's not just an item on a shelf or a service in a catalogue — it's a *promise*.

A response to a human need or a longing. Whether selling toothpaste, tech, or tea, your product must hit that emotional and functional sweet spot.

Here's where it gets interesting: when you design a product, you're not just creating something that "works." You're crafting an *experience*. And experiences stick because of how they make us *feel*. That's where sensory memory kicks in — the texture, the scent, the sound when it opens, the weight in your hand. Each little moment contributes to how your product is remembered.

Look at the iPhone — it's not just about the specs. The smooth swipe, the satisfying click, the crisp packaging. These micro-details are no accident. And Colgate? That red-and-white tube is as much about sensory recall as it is about plaque removal. The menthol hit? That's memory in action.

So, a good product doesn't just solve, it stays.

Price

Now, price. Ah, the number game, you may think, but it's much more psychological than it seems. You see, pricing is not just math; it's *meaning*. It tells your customer where you stand: affordable luxury? Premium necessity? Budget-friendly but dependable?

Neurologically speaking, the brain stores price points as memories. If you bought something for $99, the next time you see a similar product at $149, your brain automatically does a silent comparison. This is what neuroscientists call anchoring bias.

Think about Rolex. They don't just charge a premium — they anchor themselves in a certain space in your memory: craftsmanship, heritage, prestige. In FMCG, Tide detergent says, "We're premium, but you'll thank us when that stain disappears."

The experience reinforces the price memory, and price memory in turn affects the next purchase decision. So sure, pricing is a number; but it's also a memory, a feeling, and a statement.

Place

Now we come to Place, aka where and how the product meets the customer. It's not just about location; it's about accessibility and emotional ease. Can they find it when they want it? Does it feel seamless, intuitive? Here's where sensory cues come into play. The way the store smells, the lighting, and even the shelf layout influence what the brain remembers about the buying experience.

Amazon has cracked this like nobody else—it's not just fast, it's frictionless. That ease becomes part of the brand memory. Similarly, Coca-Cola is so present that it feels almost ambient. You see it everywhere—vending machines, movie halls, highway dhabas, and that ubiquity builds familiarity and recall. So, the right placement isn't just about being available—it's about being *unforgettable*.

Promotion

Promotion is your brand's voice—how it speaks to the world. Ads, content, influencers, stories—all are meant not just to inform but to embed memory. Here's the neuroscience angle: emotions are the strongest drivers of memory. So, if your promotion/ads make someone laugh, cry, or feel seen—boom, memory formed.

Coca-Cola's "Share a Coke" campaign? That wasn't just a gimmick. It personalized the experience and triggered a social-emotional loop—"This one has *my* name!" That moment gets stored in the hippocampus and retrieved at the next purchase opportunity. Dove's "Real Beauty" did the same—it challenged perceptions, tugged at heartstrings, and created an emotional hook that became part of the brand's identity. So don't just promote. *Provoke*. Create emotion. That's what sells.

People

Now, this one is deeply human. People—the ones behind your brand—the ones on the floor, on the phone, in the warehouse. The faces, voices, and gestures become the emotional interface of your brand. The brain remembers faces far more than logos.

That's why brands like Ritz-Carlton don't just train for skill; they train for empathy. Guests are not just served; they're made to feel seen, remembered, and valued. Lush Cosmetics nails this too. Their store staff aren't passive; they engage, explain, touch, and involve you in the sensory journey of the product. That human layer adds warmth and memorability.

So, if your people create joy, empathy, and connection, the brand will be affectionately remembered.

Process

Finally, the most underrated P: *Process*. It's the behind-the-scenes choreography that either delights or frustrates. These are not just operations, from app navigation to delivery flow, from returns to real-time chat. They're *emotional touchpoints*. A smooth process creates trust. A glitchy one becomes a memory, for all the wrong reasons. Think about Uber. The whole journey, from tap to track to tip, is fluid. That's not luck; intentional design feeds into process memory. Unilever does this too — from sustainable supply chains to eco-packaging, they build trust through process clarity and consistency.

Remember: the brain doesn't just store *what* happened — it stores *how* it felt.

Final Thought

The 6Ps aren't isolated boxes in a strategy doc. They're interconnected memory cues. Each one, when crafted with sensory and emotional intelligence, becomes a part of how your brand is felt, remembered, and re-purchased. When brands embed themselves in memory through sound, sight, feeling, emotion, and story, they don't just win the sale. They win the mind.

16

PRODUCT USAGE MEMORY

You know, marketers often obsess over brand logos, celebrity endorsements, and jazzy campaigns — but they sometimes forget the real battleground: *the moment someone actually uses the product.* This is where the magic—or the disappointment—truly unfolds. In neuroscience, we call this Product Usage Memory. It's not about what people think of your brand in theory, but what they feel when they open, use, and live with your product. This memory sits deep in the emotional and sensory zones of the brain, like the amygdala[3] and the hippocampus, and can be incredibly powerful in shaping repeat behavior, preference, and even brand love. Let me break it down.

What Is Product Usage Memory?

Everything happens in the customer's mind during and right after product use. From the crisp tear of a packet to the fizz of a drink to the comfort of a scent — these micro-moments are not just "nice to have." They're how brands live rent-free in people's heads.

Why does this matter? While *brand image* is built through ads and promotions, *usage memory* is built through real experiences. One is passive; the other is personal.

Let's look at a few examples. You'll see how small details become lifelong brand anchors:

- The *pop* when you open a Pringles can
- The *citrus burst* from an orange face wipe
- The *crunch* of the first chip
- The *slippery silkiness* of lotion melting into your skin
- The *lingering scent* of shampoo that travels with you all day

These aren't just features—they're *feelings*. They leave emotional residue. And once those memories are formed, they guide future purchases almost on autopilot.

How to Create Strong Product Usage Memory (Step-by-Step)

Let's now look at how to build this memory, using neuroscience and common sense intentionally.

Step 1: Identify & Map the Product Usage Journey

Before you can optimize anything, you have to *observe*, not just in a focus group. Go deep—study how real people actually use your product. Break the experience down into stages:

a. **Opening the Product:** The very first touch — how the wrapper tears, the sound it makes, the look inside — sets the tone.
b. **Using the Product:** Here's the juicy part. This is where texture, scent, visuals, sound, and performance all converge. It's the most powerful memory-making zone.
c. **Storing or Finishing:** Is the product easy to put away?
d. Does the container spill or reseal well? Is there frustration or satisfaction?
e. **After-Effect:** What remains is the scent, the feeling, the emotion. Does it bring calm? Guilt? Confidence? Whatever lingers is what gets stored.

Example – Chips (Yes, the humble snack):
- **Opening:** That satisfying crinkle of the bag.
- **Using:** Loud crunch, strong flavor, oily fingers.
- **Finishing**: Empty the bag; maybe have some regrets.
- **After-Effect:** Guilty pleasure or full-on satisfaction.

Now tell me—haven't you experienced exactly this?

Thinking of my personal experience, I can think of one product – Tolak Angin in Indonesia - which is an extraordinary product when it comes to benefit delivered, however, the experience of opening the sachet and drinking it is so messy many times I avoid using it despite wanting to have it only because of the pack opening experience.

Step 2: Layer Sensory & Emotional Triggers

The more senses you engage, the stronger the memory. This is pure neuroscience—multiple sensory signals activate different brain parts and form durable memory pathways.

Let's break it down:

a. **Visuals** - Bright packaging. Swirls in yogurt. Smooth gradients. Subtle bubbles. It's all storytelling for the eyes. And don't forget color psychology — bright = energetic, pastel = calm.

b. **Sound** - Sound builds identity. The "click" of a bottle cap. The hiss of a spray. Even the *plop* of ketchup can become iconic. Make these sounds intentional — don't leave it to chance.

c. **Touch** - Our hands are memory machines. The coolness of a gel, the density of a scrub, and the matte feel of a luxury container translate into perceived quality.

d. **Smell & Taste** - Arguably, the most emotional senses.

e. The scent of fresh laundry? Or that tangy aftertaste of a sauce? These sensations go straight to the limbic system, deep emotional memory storage.

f. **Emotion** - Don't stop at the physical. How do you want the user to *feel*? Nostalgia? Indulgence? Freshness? If you don't define it, it happens by accident—or not at all.

Example – Ariel Detergent "That clean sheet smell? That's Ariel."

Simple. Memorable. Emotional.

Step 3: Design a Signature Ritual

Humans love routine. When you give them a ritual, they build a habit. And habit is marketing gold.

Some brands have already nailed this:

- **Nutella:** The "spoon and dip" moment — it's indulgent me-time.
- **Tic Tac:** That shake, that sound — it's playful anticipation.
- **Nescafé:** Stirring that frothy top layer — it's comfort in a cup.

Make it easy:

- Show it on the pack with icons.
- Reinforce it in ads.
- Encourage it on social media.

Tip: A ritual done twice becomes a habit. A habit repeated becomes memory. So does your brand own any ritual?

Step 4: Reinforce the Experience After Use

Even the most amazing memory will fade unless you remind people. Smart brands re-trigger the memory through nudges.

Tactics:

- Subtle reminders: "Still glowing? Thank your serum."
- Refills: "80% used? Time to top up!"
- Packaging cues: "Tag us with your Sunday ritual!"
- Emails: Emotional recall — not just "buy again,"
- but "Remember how fresh you felt?"

Example – Glossier: Their email subject lines sound like friends: "That dewy glow? You know who to thank." This isn't marketing. This is memory maintenance.

Step 5: Reflect Usage Memory in Ads

Marketing shouldn't just describe the product; it should *recreate the memory of using it*.

Tactics:
- **Emotional language:**
  - "Feel the fizz again."
  - "Smell the summer."
  - "Crave that crunch?"
- **Real customer voices:**
  - "Every time I open this, I feel calm."
  - "It's my morning ritual."
- **Sensory visuals:**
  Slow-motion swirls, ASMR sound design, soft lighting—recreate the exact usage moment.

Example – Febreze: They don't show people spraying. They show the *reaction* to the scent. It's about feeling, not function.

To Wrap It Up

Your product is never just your product. It's a series of memories in the making.

If you want brand love, don't just sell. Create moments.

- Let them hear it.
- Let them touch it.
- Let them smell it.
- Let them feel something emotional while using it.

Because when people remember how your product made them *feel*, they won't just come back. They'll *miss* it when it's gone.

17

PACKAGING MEMORY

Tell me honestly—have you ever picked a product off the shelf not because you needed it, but because it just "looked right"? Well, here's a secret: almost all of us have at some point in our lives. That's not impulse buying—that's *packaging memory* in action.

While most people think packaging is just about protection or shelf appeal, neuroscience tells a different story. Packaging—its shape, colour, texture, even the way it opens—quietly sneaks into our brains, stores itself away, and shows up at the exact moment of decision-making. We call this nonverbal brand memory. It doesn't shout, it doesn't even speak, but it stays.

What Is Packaging Memory?

It's the mental snapshot your brain takes every time you interact with a product's outer form—not just how it looks but also how it feels, smells, and even sounds.

Yes, sound. Think of the "click" of a Nivea tin closing or the "pop" of a soda can. That sound is now a memory.

Some key packaging triggers:
- Shape (hello, Pringles tube)
- Colour (can you forget Tiffany Blue?)
- Texture (matte vs glossy)
- Logo and label position
- Unboxing feel
- Even scent, if it's infused!

These cues don't just help us recognize a brand. They *anchor* it in our emotional brain, especially when time is tight or attention is scattered (which is always, right?).

Why Packaging Memory Matters

Let's break it down. Multiple factors influence what the brain actually takes in when it looks at a shelf.

1. Speed – You Have Just 3–7 Seconds

Walk into any supermarket. The shelves are screaming for attention. In that chaos, your brain goes into shortcut mode—scanning for what feels familiar, not necessarily what's best.

If your packaging memory is strong, you get picked. If not, you're invisible.

Distinctive packaging = faster brain processing = faster decision = more sales.

2. Recognition – Brains Don't Read, They Scan

Let's admit it; most of us don't read labels. We scan. We spot colors, shapes, and fonts we *already know*.

This is called *visual fluency*. When your packaging design is familiar, the brain relaxes. It feels safe. That trust translates into buying behavior.

So even if your customers have no clue about the ingredients, they'll still pick your face wash because it *looks familiar*.

3. Emotion – The Real Decision-Maker

You may think people choose based on logic. But neuroscience says otherwise. *Emotions make the final call.*

The texture of a soap box, the comforting scent of an old shampoo, and the elegant gold font on a chocolate wrapper pull at your heartstrings, not your head.

Packaging that evokes pleasure, nostalgia, or even a sense of pride becomes a powerful emotional hook.

That's why some customers keep empty packs because it feels wrong to throw them away.

4. Loyalty – Repetition Creates Rituals

Packaging design becomes part of the customer's routine when it stays consistent. That exact same cereal box, the shape of that ketchup bottle, the opening flap on your favorite moisturizer—these little actions become rituals.

And rituals are remembered.

Every time you open it, you reinforce the brand memory loop — a cycle that builds loyalty without a single word spoken.

How to Build Packaging Memory (Step-by-Step)

Let's now explore how to create packaging that not only looks good but also lives in your customer's mind.

1. Start with Distinctiveness

Want to be remembered? First, be different.

Strategies:
- Unique shapes (think: Toblerone triangle)
- Signature colors (Cadbury Purple, anyone?)
- Bold, recognizable silhouettes (Absolut Vodka's bottle)

Neuromarketing Tip: The brain stores *novelty* better than sameness. If it stands out, it stays in.

2. Tap into Emotion

The best packaging design is not cold or "clean." It's *felt*.

Ways to Add Emotion:
- Soft-touch matte finish = elegance
- Hand-drawn illustrations = authenticity
- Metallic gold = luxury
- Recycled textures = sustainability

Example: Lush uses black pots with hand-written labels. It doesn't scream "glamour," but it says "care," "eco-conscious," and "human." That's emotional branding, no frills needed.

3. Use Multi-Sensory Design

Engage more than the eyes. Because memory multiplies when more senses are involved.

Sight:	Typography, shape, colour
Touch:	Material, weight, texture
Sound:	Snap of a seal, rustle of a bag
Smell:	Embedded scents (rare, but powerful!)

Brain Fact: Multi-sensory input lights up more neural circuits, creating a stronger and longer-lasting memory.

4. Build Rituals Through Repetition

Ever peeled open a foil seal on Nutella? Or opened the foil on Ferrero Rocher

These repetitive micro-actions become *mini-rituals*. And guess what? Ritual = recall.

Examples:
- Apple's slow, deliberate unboxing — it builds *anticipation*.
- Ferrero Rocher's golden wrap — it makes each bite feel *special*. Don't just design a pack. Design a *moment*.

5. Tell a Visual Story

People forget data. But they remember stories, especially visual ones.

Tips:
- Show your brand's origin or values
- Use icons or illustrations to communicate purpose

Example: Ben & Jerry's uses playful fonts, cows, and activist slogans. It's not just ice cream. It's a vibe. A story. A statement.

How to Use Packaging Memory in Marketing

Alright, now that you've crafted unforgettable packaging, how do you use it smartly?

1. Be Consistent — Always

If your packaging becomes familiar, don't mess with it. At least not dramatically.

Subtle tweaks? Sure. Revolutionary redesigns? Not unless you *want* to confuse your customers.

Heinz Ketchup looks almost identical across decades, and it works.

2. Make Packaging the Hero of Your Ads

Feature it front and center. Not as a footnote.

- Show it in motion
- Use 3D renders or slow-motion shots
- Let people *touch it* visually

Red Bull always shows its slim silver-blue can. That visual becomes the brand.

3. Think Shelf First (Even Digitally)

Even online, packaging is a *signal*. Use strong contrast, minimal text, and iconic shape.

Tools:

- Eye-tracking studies
- A/B test shelf visuals

Ask: "Which pack gets noticed first?"

Remember, you're not just fighting competitors — you're fighting attention.

4. Make Packaging Shareable

Online shopping has changed the game. Now, packaging needs to look good in photos as well. And that too on a 1 square inch on a 5-inch screen.

- Encourage unboxing content
- Add a wow moment (like Glossier's pink bubble wrap pouch)
- Tag users who share it

To people now, if the packaging is "not aesthetically pleasing," it does not serve its purpose in marketing.

5. Use It in Loyalty & Nostalgia Campaigns

Packaging can tug on heartstrings. Bring back old versions. Create limited editions. Celebrate milestones. Think: Kellogg's retro Tin Boxes. They didn't just sell a cornflake. They sold a memory.

Final Thoughts

Packaging isn't decoration. It's declaration. It's the first touchpoint, the last impression, and sometimes — the only conversation your brand has with the customer.

So, make it count. Make it feel. Make it memorable.

When people love the pack, they don't just remember the product—they *return* to it.

18

PRICING MEMORY

Let's be honest. Pricing feels like a cold, hard game of numbers, right? You set a price, the customer sees it, and they either buy or walk away. End of story? Not quite. Because in reality, *pricing is never just about the number*. It's about how that number makes people *feel*. And that feeling—whether it's "oh, this is a steal" or "hmm, that's a bit much" — is stored deep in the brain as something called *Pricing Memory*.

Now here's the kicker: once that internal reference is formed, all future prices get judged against it, not logically, but *emotionally*.

What Is Pricing Memory, Really?

It's your customer's *mental benchmark*—a subconscious idea of what something "should" cost based on past experiences and how they felt about them.

This mental benchmark doesn't appear out of thin air. It's shaped by:

- Past prices they've seen

- What competitors charge
- Previous discounts and offers
- How the price made them *feel*
- And even the story around the brand (luxury vs. budget, for example)

Once locked in, this price becomes an anchor. The brain doesn't look at your current price in isolation. It compares it to this internal standard and decides how it feels about *you*.

Why Pricing Memory Is Crucial for Marketers

Let's walk through the deeper impact of pricing memory, not in theory, but in real, everyday consumer behavior.

1. Pricing Sets the Mental Anchor

The *first* price your customer sees becomes the anchor. Everything after that gets measured against it.

So, $69 is not just $69. If it follows an "original price of $99," it feels like a deal. However, if the customer is accustomed to seeing similar products at $49, then $69 may feel expensive, even if the value is superior.

If they see:

- "Was $120, now $79" — the $120 becomes the reference
- "3-pack bundle for $39" — now anything over $13 feels pricey per item

This perception is automatic. People don't stop to recalculate or evaluate the cost-benefit. The brain reacts based on its stored anchor.

That's why it's smarter to say "Was $149" instead of just "Now $99." The contrast creates value perception.

2. Familiar Prices Build Trust

There's a reason people trust brands with stable pricing. If your favorite shampoo is *always* around $8.99, and one day it's $13.50, you hesitate. Your brain goes, "Wait... something feels off."

That discomfort can break loyalty. The pricing memory has been violated even if the product hasn't changed.

Conversely, when prices stay consistent, people start trusting you without even thinking about it. That's silent loyalty.

3. Tiny Tweaks Drive Big Conversions

Ever noticed how $4.99 feels way cheaper than $5? That's not a coincidence. That's how the brain reads numbers — from left to right.

This is called the Left-Digit Effect. The brain categorizes $4.99 in the "$4" zone, not "$5." Even a 1-cent difference changes mental categories.

You're not manipulating. You're working *with* the brain's default settings.

4. Emotions Matter More Than Math

You might think people compare prices rationally. "This is $60, that's $80 — I'll pick the cheaper one." Not always. Because the price doesn't live in a vacuum, it lives in a story.

- "This $25 self-care kit is for your peace of mind"
- "Just $1/day for the energy boost you need"
- "$149 for a gift they'll never forget"

These aren't price tags. They're *emotional frames*. And that's what makes them stick.

Brain fact: Emotionally framed prices light up the amygdala[3], the part of the brain responsible for emotional decision-making. That's where lasting pricing memory is formed.

How to Create Strong Pricing Memory (Step-by-Step)

Let's now decode how to plant the right pricing anchors into your customer's brain — and make them stay.

Step 1: Start With a High Anchor

Begin with a price that sets the tone — even if it's not the one you expect them to choose.

Strategies:

- Mention the "original" price before the discounted one
- Introduce a "premium" tier even if most won't buy it
- Use comparison pricing: "Others sell for $89 — we're $59"

Example: Apple announces the $1,199 Pro Max model first, so when you see the $899 version, it suddenly feels "affordable."

Step 2: Use Charm Pricing (It Still Works!)

$9.99, $39, $4.95 — these are *not* accidents. These are pricing cues crafted to nudge perception.

The brain subconsciously thinks $9.99 is in the "$9 zone," even though it's a cent away from $10.

Use this across:
- Product pricing
- Subscription plans
- Bundled offers

The difference between $199 and $200 may be $1 on paper, but it's *psychologically massive*.

Step 3: Tie the Price to an Emotion

People don't just remember *how much* they paid. They remember *how it made them feel*.

So reframe your pricing like this:
- "Just $2 a day for better sleep"
- "$49 for peace of mind"
- "$19 to spoil yourself this Sunday"

That's when price stops being a number and becomes an *emotional investment*.

Step 4: Reinforce the Price Across Channels

The more your customers see a price, the more "normal" it feels. This is called *price fluency*.

So, echo it on:
- Your website
- Product packaging
- Instagram ads
- SMS reminders
- Loyalty emails

Neural pathway: Repetition reinforces memory formation in the *hippocampus*.

If it occurs often enough, it becomes familiar, and familiarity = safety = *purchase*.

Step 5: Use Bundling to Reshape Perception

When you sell items in a bundle, people stop doing the math. They assess *total value* instead.

Examples:
- "Bundle: Cleanser + Toner + Moisturizer — $49"
- "Family Pack: 4 boxes for $25"
- "$99 Wellness Kit (worth $145 separately)"

Now the brain focuses on *savings*, not on individual item costs. That's a pricing memory *reset*.

How to Use Pricing Memory in Marketing Campaigns

Once your audience has seen or felt your price, how do you keep that memory alive?

1. Trigger Memory With Anchors in Ads
- "Was $149. Now $89."
- "Still just $9.99 after 10 years."
- "Same great value. No price hike in 5 years."

This reactivates the pricing anchor, especially for returning or repeat customers.

2. Frame Discounts as Personal Gains

Instead of just saying "Save $20," try:
- "You keep $20 in your pocket."
- "That's $0.66 a day — less than your morning coffee"
- "For $1/day, you get your glow back."

The price becomes a *gift*, not a cost.

3. Reward Loyalty With Price Recognition

Pricing memory also builds loyalty. So acknowledge it.
- "Your rate is locked at $49 — thanks for sticking with us."
- "Early supporters always get 15% off."
- "We remember you. Your price hasn't changed."

These messages show that *you remember their pricing memory, which* builds emotional equity.

4. Upsell and Cross-Sell Based on Stored Price Anchors

Once your base price is stored — say $59 — use that to introduce upgrades:

- "Just $10 more for deluxe"
- "Add $5 and get 2x the volume"
- "Upgrade to premium for $20 extra"

The anchor makes every add-on *feel like a bargain*.

5. Retarget Using the Same Price Cue

Let's say a visitor saw your product at $79 but didn't buy. Retarget with:

- "Still thinking? It's still $79."
- "Your $79 favorite is waiting — limited stock"

The familiar price reignites the original feeling. You're not selling — you're *reminding*.

The brain doesn't remember the best price. It remembers the *most emotionally satisfying* price.

So as a brand, your job is not to just "price it right" — but to make that price feel good, feel fair, and most importantly... *feel remembered*. That's the power of Pricing Memory.

19

PROMOTION MEMORY

Here's a little truth bomb: people don't always buy the best product. They buy the one they *remember*. Now think about that. You might have the most brilliant shampoo, the tastiest cookie, or the most budget-friendly subscription. But if your ad doesn't *stick* in the mind, you'll be forgotten faster than yesterday's headlines. That's where Promotion Memory comes into play. It's not just about running ads—it's about creating *mental real estate* in the brain.

Two Kinds of Ad Memory: Explicit vs Implicit

Let's simplify the neuroscience a bit:

Memory Type	What it is	How it works
Explicit Memory	Conscious recall	"I saw that Coca-Cola ad yesterday."
Implicit Memory	Subconscious feeling	"This brand just *feels* familiar and trustworthy."

Here's the twist: even if people *don't remember seeing your ad*, it may still *influence their behavior*. That's how powerful implicit memory is.

Neuro insight: Emotional, surprising, and sensory-rich ads are more likely to be encoded into *long-term memory*, especially if repeated consistently.

How the Brain Stores Advertising

To get remembered, an ad needs to do four things:

1. Grab Attention (Sensory Cortex Activation)

The human brain is constantly filtering out noise. If your ad doesn't stand out in the first few seconds, it's toast.

Ways to hook attention:
- Bold visuals
- Unexpected sound or silence
- Surprising movement
- Irregular ad format (e.g., vertical, split-screen, cinemograph)

Think of that moment when you scroll past a hundred videos, and suddenly one makes you *stop*. That's your sensory cortex lighting up.

2. Trigger Emotion (Amygdala Engagement)

Emotion is the glue of memory. If your ad doesn't make people *feel*, it won't make them *remember*.

Emotions that work especially well:
- Joy and laughter
- Nostalgia
- Awe
- Warmth and empathy
- A touch of fear (used wisely)

Example: Google's "Parisian Love" ad — a story told entirely through search queries — melts hearts in under a minute. Simple, human, unforgettable.

3. Build Associations (Hippocampus Encoding)

The hippocampus is the memory librarian of the brain.

It stores new memories by linking them to *what we already know*.

That's why:
- Ads that use pop culture cues, everyday life, or cultural references are easier to recall
- Storytelling helps us *relate* and file it under "things I care about."

"Dumb Ways to Die" wasn't just catchy. It became a *mental category* of fun + safety.

4. Use Repetition (Strengthen Neural Pathways)

Want to get remembered? Say it again. And again. And again — but smartly.

Repetition doesn't mean boredom. It means:
- Repeating visual motifs
- Reinforcing your slogan
- Using the same jingle, tone, or brand voice

This repetition turns short-term memory into long-term recall by creating strong neural imprints, especially when delivered across multiple platforms.

How to Create Memorable Advertising (Step-by-Step)

Let's now build out the blueprint.

Step 1: Emotion Is Your Superpower

Forget features. Focus on feelings. Craft ads that tap into:
- Family
- Belonging
- Pride
- Self-worth
- Wonder
- Laughter

Example: Thai Life Insurance ads are masterclasses in emotional storytelling — sad, beautiful, and wildly shareable.

Emotional content stimulates the amygdala[3], which tags the memory as "important" and makes it stick.

Step 2: Be Visually Distinct

What's one thing all memorable ads have in common? They don't look like the rest.

Ways to break the pattern:
- Colour schemes that pop
- Unexpected camera angles
- Silent ads in a noisy feed
- Hand-drawn animations

Think: Old Spice's "The Man Your Man Could Smell Like" — no one saw it coming, and everyone remembered it.

Step 3: Anchor Sensory Cues

Sensory memories are powerful because they *bypass logic* and go straight to the emotional brain.

Here's how to plug in different senses:

Sense	Application in Ads
Sight	Vibrant visuals, iconic logo
Sound	Sonic logos, jingles, and tone of voice
Emotion	Facial expressions, body language, storytelling
Rhythm	Rhyme, music, and pacing for flow

Intel's 5-note sonic logo doesn't even need a visual — you *hear* it and recall the brand.

Step 4: Craft a Simple, Repeatable Message

Too many brands try to be too clever. But what actually works? *Simplicity.*

- A short, punchy slogan
- A single core message
- One strong image or CTA

Nike's "Just Do It" is 3 words long — and globally unforgettable.

In India, "Kya Chal Raha hai" - "FOG chal raha hai" from Deodorant brand FOG created a simple repeatable message which became Viral and skyrocketed the brand sales

Step 5: Add Characters or Narratives

Stories are easier to remember than facts. Characters create continuity and emotional familiarity.

Tactics:
- Use mascots or spokespeople
- Create episodic ad series
- Build mini story arcs across platforms

The M&M's characters are not just mascots — they're memory triggers. Stories activate the Default Mode Network in the brain — the same part we use when imagining, daydreaming, or remembering life events.

Step 6: Repeat Across Platforms

Consistency is memory's best friend. When people encounter the same elements in multiple places, the memory gets reinforced.

Use:
- The same voice and music on TV, YouTube, Spotify
- Similar visuals in Instagram, packaging, and website
- Core message across billboards, app notifications, and retargeting ads.

How to Reinforce Promotion Memory in Your Marketing

Once your ad is live, the work isn't over. Now you *embed* the memory.

1. Retarget Using Familiar Visuals and Audio

The best retargeting ads don't introduce something new. They repeat *exactly* what worked — same sound, colors, language.
- "Still thinking about it?"
- "That dewy glow? It's just $29 away."
- "Don't forget your first love (of coffee)!"

Even when entering new markets, Coca-Cola never changes its red and white palette.

2. Build Episodic Campaigns

Treat your ad like a TV series. Build anticipation.
- Part 1: The problem
- Part 2: The breakthrough
- Part 3: The transformation

John Lewis' holiday ads in the UK are tearjerkers — people *wait for them* each year. That's emotional advertising done right.

In India, Amul takes a current affairs issue and creates a Billboard which has become iconic and everyone looks forward to every next release

3. Encourage the Audience to Remix the Memory
The best ads today? They're co-created, Encourage:
- User-generated content
- Challenges or memes
- Re-creation of your story, dance, or slogan

When users replicate your ad's voice, rhythm, or emotion, it becomes their own memory.

4. Use Ad Memory to Support Pricing and Brand Loyalty
A remembered ad = higher perceived value.
- Brands with emotional ad recall can charge more
- Familiar ads reduce the need for "explanation"
- The emotional echo justifies the price

Studies show that brands with high advertising recall enjoy more price elasticity and stronger repurchase behavior.

Advertisement Memory = Long-Term Brand Recall

Component	Memory Trigger
Emotion	Deep encoding via the amygdala
Distinctiveness	Dopamine-driven attention
Sensory Anchors	Multisensory memory traces
Storytelling	Episodic memory activation
Repetition	Neural pathway reinforcement

In the age of 3-second attention spans and constant noise, *forgettable is fatal.* The brands that win aren't the loudest — they're the ones that leave a mark on the brain.

So the next time you create an ad, ask yourself:
- Will this make someone *feel* something?
- Will they *remember* it a week later?
- Will it pop into their head the next time they're at the shelf?
- Because in marketing, it's not about being the best — it's about being the *most remembered.*

20

PEOPLE MEMORY

Think back for a moment. Have you ever returned to a salon *just* because the stylist remembered your last haircut? Or stayed loyal to a doctor *because* they looked you in the eye and explained everything calmly?

Or recommended a brand to your friends simply because *someone* from the company went out of their way to help you? That's not luck.

That's People Memory. And in service-heavy industries — hospitality, wellness, healthcare, retail, even banking — this is *everything*. It's not just about what people buy. It's about *who* they remember and *how those people made them feel.*

What Is People Memory?

People Memory is the emotional imprint customers form about the humans behind your brand.

It includes:

- The barista who knows your name

- The support agent who solved your issue without scripts.
- The delivery guy who smiled and said, "Have a great day."
- The Relationship Manager from the bank who did not try to oversell and gave you honest advice.
- Even the founder's video on the "About Us" page

We don't just remember what was said. We remember *how it felt to be treated.*

The Neuroscience of People Memory

Let's peek inside the brain.

- **Amygdala** – Processes emotional significance. This is where "they were so kind" or "that guy was rude" gets stored.
- **Medial Prefrontal Cortex** – Helps us make social judgments. It evaluates empathy, warmth, and trustworthiness.
- **Fusiform Gyrus** – Specializes in facial recognition. That's why we remember faces way more than facts or numbers.
- **Mirror Neurons** – Fire when we see someone smile, laugh, or care. They *make us feel* what others feel. That's how empathy gets stored in memory. That's what makes us cry when we see a sad movie

So, when a hotel concierge anticipates your need without being asked? When a teacher remembers your child's nickname, that's not just service. That's brand loyalty, rooted in memory.

Why People Memory Matters in Marketing

Let's make this real.

1. Human Connection Builds Emotional Trust

No matter how tech-savvy your business is, customers crave *human energy*. One warm interaction with a real person can outweigh five ads.

One helpful reply on Twitter can rescue a poor experience.
You can't automate empathy — but you can train for it.

2. Faces Are More Memorable Than Logos

People recognize faces faster than fonts. We're wired that way. So, showing the people behind the brand makes your company seem more real, trustworthy, and relatable.

That's why brands like Glossier and Zappos put *people's stories in* the front and center. It's not just about the product. It's about the *person who gave it to you.*

3. Positive People Memory Creates Advocacy

Happy customers *talk about people*. Not just the brand.

- "That customer service representative was so patient."
- "The chef came out to check on us!"
- "Their rep stayed late just to help."

These stories fuel *word of mouth* — the most powerful marketing there is.

How to Create Strong People Memory (Step-by-Step)

Let's get into the "how."

Step 1: Train for Empathy, Not Just Efficiency

Yes, speed matters. But warmth stays.

Train your teams to:

- Listen without interrupting
- Personalize the interaction ("How's the baby doing now?")
- Use positive micro-expressions (eye contact, a smile, relaxed posture)

Empathy activates the amygdala[3] and mirror neurons, creating emotionally rich memories.

Step 2: Make Faces Part of Your Brand

Showcase your people. Literally.

- Add "Meet the Team" on your site
- Use real staff in ads and Reels
- Share behind-the-scenes stories

Airbnb does this brilliantly; it puts hosts' faces on every listing. You don't book a room; you connect with a person.

Step 3: Create Signature Human Rituals

Make your brand's human interactions *distinctive and repeatable*.

Examples:
- Chick-fil-A staff always say: "My pleasure."
- Ritz-Carlton: "Ladies and gentlemen serving ladies and gentlemen."
- Starbucks: Writes your name on the cup (sometimes hilariously wrong — but memorable!)

Language, tone, greeting rituals — they all become memory triggers.

Step 4: Empower Staff to Create Delight Moments

Give your team permission to go off-script and surprise people.
- A handwritten thank-you note
- A "just because" sample tucked into the box
- A personal follow-up message after a service

These micro-gestures often become *the story* customers tell.

"I don't remember what I bought, but I remember how they made me feel." — That's the goal.

Step 5: Publicly Celebrate Your People

Recognition should not stay internal.
- Spotlight team members on social media
- Share customer reviews that name staff
- Tell the stories of the people who make your brand what it is.

This builds *parasocial bonds* — customers feel they know your team before they even interact.

Step 6: Build Relationship Continuity

The more customers see the same person, the stronger the memory.
- Assign dedicated account managers
- Let customers book appointments with "their" stylist, banker, or coach

- Offer continuity in service — even digitally (e.g., chat with "Sarah from Support")

Relationships reduce friction. Familiar faces build confidence.

How to Use People Memory in Your Marketing

Now, how do you amplify this beautiful, human magic?

1. Turn Staff Into Brand Ambassadors

Don't hide your team. Let them be the face of your message.

- "Sarah's skincare tips"
- "Meet Jason, the trainer behind our workouts."
- "Why Emma picked this blend for your morning coffee"

When people trust the *person*, they trust the *brand* more.

2. Invite Human-Centric Testimonials

Ask your customers to recall *who* helped them, not just *what* they bought.

- "Amanda made my day."
- "Ben was like talking to a friend."
- "Shoutout to Priya who walked me through everything!"

Names + feelings = sticky stories = brand gold.

3. Use Real Staff in Content, Not Stock Models

Show the real faces behind your business. Especially for service industries.

- Real people in explainer videos
- Actual customer support agents in the FAQs
- "Signed by" emails that show the name, role, and a photo

"From Kayla at Support" hits differently than "Customer Care Team."

4. Personalize Follow-Ups With Memory Cues

Use your CRM wisely.

- "Hey Mia, same stylist as last time — ready when you are."

- "Alex, your skin profile is still on file. Want to reorder?"
- "Dr. Mehta is available for your next session next week."

You're not just reaching out — you're *rekindling a memory*.

5. Gamify Staff Recognition

Celebrate great service, publicly.

- Let customers vote for "Hero of the Month"
- Create a digital "Wall of Wow" on your website
- Share love notes and reviews as stories

Not only does this motivate your team, but it also reminds your customers *who* they loved.

People don't remember your business by the button on your app or the colour of your logo. They remember the *humanness* they felt — the eye contact, the empathy, the care. So train it. Show it. Celebrate it.

Because your biggest brand differentiator isn't always your product or your price.

It's the *people* they'll remember long after the product is used.

21

PROCESS MEMORY

Let's play out two real-world scenarios.
You order something online. Site loads instantly. Checkout takes two clicks. You get a confirmation in 5 seconds. The delivery arrives *a day early*. Neatly packed. No mess-ups. No drama. Now compare that to this:

Website glitches. You have to enter your card details twice. No confirmation email. Three days later, you're still refreshing your tracking link. Customer service says, "We'll get back to you."

Ugh.

You didn't just experience a delay. You formed a memory. That, dear reader, is *Process Memory*.

What Is Process Memory?
It's the emotional and sensory imprint formed by your brand's flow—the way things work, move, respond, and feel from the customer's point of view. Not the product. Not the promotion.

But the *path* they walked to get to your brand and *through* it.

And here's the thing — even if the product is great, a clunky or frustrating process *damages* your brand memory. Conversely, a smooth, seamless process becomes a *silent trust builder*. In the brain, ease = pleasure. Friction = stress.

Both get stored. One creates loyalty. The other creates churn.

Why Process Memory Matters

Let's break this down.

1. Experience Is the Product

In today's world, the *delivery* of the product is just as important as the product itself.

You're not just selling coffee — you're selling the ease of ordering it, the clarity of instructions, the speed of the delivery, and the way it's handed over.

Every little touchpoint is either *easing friction* or *adding to it*.

And guess what? The *feelings* generated by those micro-moments become *the brand* in your customer's head.

It's not just "Did it work?" — it's "How did it make me feel while it worked?"

2. The Brain Loves Flow

Our brains are naturally wired for fluency — the smoother something feels, the more trustworthy it seems.

So when:

- Navigation is intuitive
- Service is responsive
- Delivery is predictable
- Instructions are clear
- Returns are simple

the brain doesn't just relax. It *rewards* you. With repeat business. With referrals. With love.

3. Friction Creates Negative Emotional Tags

Every point of confusion, every extra step, every "Sorry, please try again later" adds an emotional tag to the memory.

And emotional tags are what the brain uses when making future decisions.

That one error message at checkout?

That confusing sign-up form?

It may have cost you *way more* than a lost sale.

It may have cost you trust.

How to Create Positive Process Memory (Step-by-Step)

Let's get practical.

Step 1: Map the End-to-End Experience

Start by breaking your customer's journey into steps — not just the visible parts, but everything they go through from first click to final interaction.

Map moments like:

- First impression (loading speed, homepage clarity)
- Discovery (search, filters, FAQs)
- Purchase or booking
- Fulfillment (delivery, shipping, onboarding)
- After-sales (returns, feedback, reminders)

Where are the speed bumps?

Where do people hesitate?

Where do you ask too much, too fast?

This map is your emotional blueprint.

Step 2: Prioritize Friction Removal

Not all process memories are about delight. Sometimes, just *removing frustration* is enough.

Quick wins:

- Reduce clicks.
- Minimize data entry.
- Pre-fill known information.
- Clarify jargon.
- Offer human help *before* they rage-quit.

Less cognitive load = higher satisfaction.

And satisfaction is the foundation of memory.

Step 3: Add Micro-Moments of Joy

Once the basics are smooth, sprinkle delight.

Ideas:
- "Woohoo! You're almost done" messages
- Fun loading animations
- Encouraging tone of voice ("We've got you!")
- Little sound cues or haptic taps in apps
- Surprise freebies or notes

These create *emotional spikes* — little bursts of positivity that the brain locks onto.

Duolingo's owl is encouraging you to finish a lesson? That's a joyful process nudge.

Step 4: Design for Predictability

The brain hates uncertainty. It wants to *know* what's next. So communicate clearly:
- Delivery windows
- Refund policies
- Timelines for responses
- Confirmation messages after every action

Don't make your customer wonder, "Is this working?"

Make them feel, "Oh, I know exactly what's happening."

Step 5: Humanize Automation

Automated doesn't have to feel robotic. Add a human touch.

Examples:
- Friendly email headers: "Hi Alex, we're packing your order!"
- Progress bars with personality: "Almost there… tea's nearly steeped!"
- Customer support that says, "We hear you — let's fix this."

Even bots can feel human if you write them with *care*.

Step 6: Test With Real Humans

Don't assume your flow works — *watch people use it.*

Sit with real users or customers and observe:
- Where do they pause?

- What confuses them?
- What brings a smile?

Then *refine ruthlessly*. Because *a smoother experience = a stronger memory = a more lovable brand.*

How to Use Process Memory in Your Marketing

Alright, the process is smooth. Now, how do you *amplify* that as a brand asset?

1. Market the Experience, Not Just the Product

Tell people *how easy* your service is.

- "Delivered in 2 days — every time."
- "3-step booking, zero waiting."
- "Happiness, in one click."

Let the *process* be your USP.

2. Capture Process Stories from Customers

Encourage reviews that highlight experience, not just outcomes. Examples:

- "So fast — I placed the order in 1 minute!"
- "The return process was *so* smooth."
- "Loved the little message they sent me post-purchase."

Turn these into testimonials, Instagram stories, or even ads.

3. Include Process Screens in Demos & Ads

Show, don't tell.

- Screen recordings of checkout
- Unboxing moments
- Email flows
- App UI walkthroughs

When people *see* a smooth process, they believe it's effortless — even before they try it.

4. Share "Behind-the-Scenes" Operations Content

Lift the curtain.

- How your logistics team ships in 24 hours
- How your tech support resolves issues under 15 minutes

- How your onboarding flow was redesigned based on user feedback

This builds *process credibility* — a subtle but powerful trust driver.

5. Use Process Memory to Deepen Loyalty

Remind repeat customers of *how easy* it was last time.
- "Welcome back — your details are saved."
- "One-click reorder is ready!"
- "Your usual? We've got it."

Ease becomes a reason to *stay*. People might forget what they ordered. They might forget how much they paid.

But they'll *never forget* how seamless — or stressful — the experience felt. That's the legacy your process leaves behind.

So optimize it. Simplify it. Humanize it. Because the better your process feels, the better your brand is remembered.

And in the end, that's all that truly matters.

PART 8:
MARKETING RESEARCH REINVENTED USING NEURO
Measuring What the Brain Feels, Not Just Says

22

WHY TRADITIONAL RESEARCH METHODS ARE NOT ENOUGH

Let's start with a little truth bomb—most marketing research is still riding the old-school bus. Now, don't get me wrong. Traditional methods like surveys, focus groups, and interviews have served us well over the years. They've been the bread and butter of brand strategy meetings, boardroom pitches, and campaign post-mortems.

But in today's fast-evolving world, where emotions are the silent puppet masters behind consumer choices, these age-old tools can only take us so far. Why? Because they mostly rely on what people *say*, not necessarily what they *feel* deep down.

The Usual Suspects: Traditional Methods

Let's unpack this a bit.

Surveys and questionnaires? Super scalable and great for quantitative data. Want to track brand recall, purchase intent, or satisfaction levels? These tools get the job done.

You send out a form, crunch some numbers, plot a few graphs, and voila! But here's the kicker—people often tell you what they think you want to hear. Or worse, what they believe *they* should feel.

Focus groups? Ah, yes, those roundtable chats with strangers sipping coffee and debating a new logo. They offer rich emotional insights, sure, but groupthink is real. One dominant voice can sway the entire discussion. And let's not forget how polite we Indians (and frankly, many cultures) can be—we don't always want to say something negative, especially in front of others.

Then there are **in-depth interviews**. These are like friendly therapy sessions. You go deep into a person's motivations, fears, and desires. They're great for nuance but slow, resource-heavy, and tough to scale.

Observational research, on the other hand, involves researchers just watching—either in stores, homes, or controlled environments. This approach has an edge because it captures what people do, not what they say they do. But again, there's a catch: the *Hawthorne effect*. When people know they're being watched, they behave differently. It's like suddenly becoming a saint when the teacher's looking.

So, What's the Real Problem?

All these methods rely, to a large extent, on *self-reporting*. And here's where the plot thickens. Much of our decision-making as consumers isn't even conscious. We don't always know why we chose one brand over another, or why that jingle from a detergent ad gave us the feels. Asking someone to explain it is like asking a fish to describe water.

And memory? Oh boy. Human memory is messy. Ask someone what they bought last week, and chances are they'll guess. Not out of malice, but because our brains fill in the gaps without us even realizing.

Enter Neuroscience: The New Frontier

This is where neuroscience-based marketing research steps in—not with a clipboard, but with brainwaves, eye patterns, micro-expressions, and subconscious reactions. It's like turning on a flashlight in a dark room full of hidden motivations.

Let me quickly introduce you to four of the big players in this neuro-research world (we'll deep dive into each in the next chapters):

1. Electroencephalography (EEG): This is listening to your brain's electrical symphony. EEG picks up your brainwaves in real-time, so we can actually track what grabs your attention, what excites you, and what bores your senses. Brands use this to test ads, packaging, and even music.

2. Eye-tracking: This tells us where people look, what grabs their visual attention, what they skip, and how their eyes travel across a screen or shelf. It is brilliant for understanding layout, packaging, or website design.

3. Facial Coding: Have you ever seen someone say, "I love it," while their face clearly says, "meh?" Facial coding deciphers micro-expressions—those fleeting facial movements we can't control—to gauge genuine emotional responses.

4. Implicit Association Testing[7] (IAT): Here, we measure the speed with which someone links concepts in their mind. Like how quickly someone connects a brand with "trust" or "luxury." The faster the link, the stronger the subconscious association.

Traditional Tools vs. Neuroscience: What's the Real Deal?

Let's examine some key areas where traditional methods often fail and how neuroscience fills those gaps.

1. **Self-Report Dependency:** Let's face it—most traditional research depends on what people *say*. But people lie. Not always intentionally. Sometimes, to be socially acceptable, sometimes because they genuinely don't know what's going on inside their own minds or as basic as not remembering what is being asked for, **Neuro Advantage:** EEG and eye-tracking skip the verbal layer. They tap into raw, unfiltered responses that don't need a spoken explanation.

2. **Poor Emotional Resolution**: Emotions are the secret sauce behind buying behavior. Yet traditional surveys often reduce them to checkboxes—happy, sad, angry. Real emotion is way messier. **Neuro Advantage:** Tools like EEG and facial coding capture split-second emotional shifts. You get the real emotion, not just their justified responses.
3. **Unnatural Environments:** Specifically for Shopper understanding, interviews with shoppers and focus groups are often far removed from the real world. People behave differently under observation. **Neuro Advantage:** Mobile EEGs, Wearable Eye trackers, and real-world testing setups let you gather data in actual stores, where real decisions happen.
4. **Groupthink in Focus Groups:** We've all been there. One loud participant hijacks the discussion, and suddenly everyone agrees. Peer pressure is real. **Neuro Advantage:** EEG and other neuro tools collect data individually, bypassing group dynamics and capturing authentic, personal responses.
5. **Delayed Feedback:** By the time traditional methods gather feedback, the moment has passed. Emotions fade, memories get fuzzy. **Neuro Advantage:** Real-time data capture means we don't miss the moment of impact. We know exactly what a consumer felt *as* it happened.
6. **Low Predictive Power:** People often say one thing and do another. "Yes, I'll definitely buy this" doesn't always translate to action. **Neuro Advantage:** Neural engagement and emotional resonance are actually *better* predictors of future behavior than verbal promises.
7. **Language and Culture Barriers**: Surveys need to be translated, adapted, and reworded for different regions. And still, cultural nuances slip through the cracks. **Neuro Advantage:** Brain responses are universal. They transcend language. This makes neuroscience-based methods ideal for global, cross-cultural studies.

Use a Hybrid Approach to Enhance the Overall Understanding

Look, traditional research isn't going away—and it shouldn't. It still has immense value. But to truly understand the *why* behind consumer behavior, we need to go deeper than what people are willing (or able) to tell us.

That's where neuroscience steps in—not to replace the old methods, but to enhance them. Many savvy brands today use a hybrid approach: traditional tools to get the "what," and neuro-tools to understand the "why."

Because when it comes to decoding the human brain, especially in the messy, emotional world of marketing, surface-level answers just aren't enough anymore.

23

EEG (ELECTROENCEPHALOGRAM)

"The brain speaks... if you're willing to listen."

Let me tell you a story.

A global snack brand—massive, household name—just wrapped production on what they thought was their next blockbuster TV ad. It had everything: a catchy jingle, a celebrity cameo, bold visuals, and a heartwarming storyline. The focus groups had loved it. Survey scores were through the roof. The marketing team was so confident that they had already booked the most expensive ad slots during a major sporting event. All systems go.

And then...thud.

The ad aired, but nothing really happened. No spike in sales. No buzz. Brand recall? Dismal. Even social media, which normally explodes after these things, went quiet within days.

Everyone was confused. This was *supposed* to be the hit of the season.

In desperation, they turned to neuromarketing and ran an EEG study. And what they discovered was eye-opening.

It turns out that the ad did not have a great beginning. The initial 10 seconds were very boring, and hence, while in the research setting, consumers were forced to see the full ad.

In real life, most consumers switched their screens or attention within those first 10 seconds and thus did not get exposed to the most impactful part.

Focus groups didn't catch this. Why? Because they were forced to see the full ad, and they reacted based on the overall impression, which was not replicated in real life. In real life, you cannot put a gun to the consumer's head and ask them to see the entire advertisement.

Armed with this data, the brand re-edited the ad. They shortened the intro, made it more engaging, brought the product forward, and shortened the ad.

And *that* made all the difference.

This right here is why EEG is such a powerful tool in marketing. It bypasses politeness. It cuts through opinion. It listens straight to the source: the brain.

So, What Exactly Is EEG?

EEG—or Electroencephalography—is a method of recording electrical activity in the brain. Think of it as a window into what your brain is feeling, moment by moment.

Whether you're watching an ad, walking into a store, or trying out a product, your brain is constantly firing signals. EEG picks up on those.

In marketing, we use EEG to track real-time engagement, emotional arousal, attention, and mental effort, without relying on what someone *says*. Because remember: consumers don't always know what they feel. But their brain does.

The Evolution of EEG in Marketing: From Bulky Labs to Sleek Headsets

Let's take a quick journey through time.

1. The Lab Era – Early Days of EEG in Marketing

Back in the early 2000s, using EEG for marketing research was a bit like launching a rocket. You needed complex machines, gel-based electrodes, clinical settings, and trained neuroscientists. Companies like Neuro-Insight and EmSense were among the early pioneers. They strapped participants with 32 or even 128 electrodes, trying to capture reactions to TV ads, packaging, store layouts—you name it.

The insights were gold. Researchers could detect exactly when an ad sparked attention, triggered emotion, or created a memory imprint.

But boy, was it heavy. Literally and figuratively. The equipment was expensive, intrusive, and slow to set up. And let's be honest—it didn't exactly scream "real-world scenario." Participants sat in sterile labs with wires poking out of their heads. Useful? Yes. Scalable? Not at all.

2. The 2010s – Portable EEG Changes the Game

Then came the wearable tech revolution. And suddenly, EEG stepped out of the lab and into the real world.

Enter dry electrodes (no sticky gels!), Bluetooth connectivity, battery-powered, lightweight headsets. Brands like Emotiv, Muse, and NeuroSky made it possible to collect brain data in retail stores, homes, offices—basically, wherever real life happens.

These newer systems offered 8 to 14 channels—plenty to track attention, engagement, and emotional intensity. You lost some spatial precision, but the tradeoff was worth it. Now, brands could run EEG studies during live product trials, in-store activations, or digital browsing sessions.

The best part? These devices could be combined with other tools, like eye-tracking or facial coding, to create a full 360-degree view of the consumer experience.

3. The Real Disruptor – Single-Node EEG Devices

And just when we thought EEG couldn't get more accessible, along came the single-node EEG revolution.

These minimalist headsets utilize just one or two electrodes, often placed on the forehead (specifically, the prefrontal cortex). That's the area of the brain responsible for decision-making, emotional control, and attention. Which, let's be honest, is *exactly* what marketers care about.

Brands like MyndPlay and Neuroelectrics made this tech so compact that you could slip it on like a headband. And just like that, EEG became affordable even for startups, UX designers, and creative agencies.

What can a single-node EEG track?

- Attention
- Engagement
- Cognitive load (mental effort)
- Emotional valence (positive/negative feeling)

And here's the kicker: It all happens in real-time.

Why Marketers Love Single-Node EEG

- It democratizes neuroscience. Even small brands can afford to run brain-based research now.
- Perfect for A/B testing. Want to know which ad works better? Just track the brainwaves.
- Real-time feedback. Imagine changing your ad *on the fly* based on actual brain responses.
- Plug-and-play with other tools. Combine with surveys, eye-tracking, or facial coding to get layered insights.

Of course, it's not perfect.

- You don't get spatial detail, so you know *when* something's happening in the brain, not exactly *where*.
- With fewer data points, noise can sneak in more easily.

- And for deep neuroscience (like studying memory encoding across brain regions), it's not enough.

But for marketers? It's a total win. Single-node EEG gives you speed, simplicity, and just enough precision to make smarter, faster decisions.

From Raw Signals to Real Insights: How EEG Data Gets Processed

Here's what actually happens behind the scenes:

1. Raw Brain Signal

The device captures a continuous stream of voltage data (in microvolts), sampled hundreds of times per second. It's messy—full of blinks, twitches, and background noise.

2. Signal Cleaning

Before making sense of anything, signals are cleaned.

- **Bandpass filtering:** Keeps only brain-relevant frequencies (0.5–45 Hz).
- **Notch filtering:** Removes electrical interference (50/60 Hz from power lines).
- **Artifact removal:** Gets rid of noise from eye blinks and muscle movement.
- **Baseline correction:** Aligns the data to a neutral state, so we can spot shifts.
- **Smoothening**: Moving Averages are sometimes used to smooth the data to make it easier to interpret.

3. Frequency Band Analysis

Next, the cleaned signal is broken down into different brainwave bands:

- **Delta (0.5–4 Hz):** Deep unconscious state
- **Theta (4–8 Hz):** Creativity, calmness
- **Alpha (8–12 Hz):** Focused relaxation
- **Beta (12–30 Hz):** Active thinking, concentration
- **Gamma (30–100 Hz):** High-level cognition, insight

Different combinations of these tell us what's really going on inside someone's head.

4. Deriving Psychological Metrics

Proprietary algorithms convert these waves into easy-to-understand metrics:

Metric	Brain Activity	What It Means
Attention	High beta, low theta	The viewer is alert and focused
Engagement	Balanced alpha-beta	Indicates emotional involvement
Meditation	High alpha + theta	Calm and relaxed state
Cognitive Load	High beta, low alpha	The viewer is mentally working hard

These metrics are refreshed every second or two, so you can actually map emotional and cognitive flow across an entire video or experience.

The New Age of EEG in Marketing

Gone are the days when neuroscience was locked inside labs. With portable, user-friendly EEG systems, even single-node devices, we can now track the *real* consumer journey, thought by thought, emotion by emotion.

When paired with tools like AI & eye-tracking, you're not just reading what the consumer says. You're reading their *mind.*

24

EYE TRACKING

"If the eyes are windows to the soul, they're also windows into the consumer's mind."

Let me paint a picture for you.

A well-known brand (sorry, can't name them—NDAs!) had launched a new product that the marketing team was super excited about. They'd done their homework: consumer testing, packaging trials, even pre-launch buzz was strong. Everything looked perfect—on paper.

But when the product finally hit store shelves, nothing happened. There was no movement. It just sat there, collecting dust.

Desperate to figure out what was happening, the team tried something different. They fitted a few shoppers with wearable glasses equipped with—you guessed it—eye-tracking technology.

And the results? Eye-opening (literally).

Most shoppers didn't even *see* the product. Their attention kept drifting to the brighter promotional displays nearby.

Despite being technically "well-positioned," the new item was practically invisible. That's when it hit them: you can't sell what people don't notice. And this is the power of eye-tracking. It tells us where people *actually* look, not where we *assume* they're looking. And when you're competing for a consumer's attention in a visual jungle of packaging, screens, and banners, that's priceless.

So, What Is Eye-Tracking?

At its core, eye-tracking is exactly what it sounds like—it tracks eye movements. But more than that, it tells us:
- Where people are looking
- How long they've been looking
- The order in which they move their gaze

In marketing, this data becomes gold. Whether it's an ad, a product shelf, a website, or a mobile app, eye-tracking shows you what catches attention... and what gets ignored. Perhaps most importantly, it captures subconscious visual behavior. People don't always realize what they look at or how long they stare at something, but their eyes do. They remember.

Types of Eye-Tracking Devices

Depending on the research setup, different tools are used to track eye movements. Let's go through the major types:

1. Screen-Based Trackers

These are typically mounted below or around a screen, like a laptop, mobile phone, or tablet. They track how users interact with digital content, such as websites, ads, videos, or apps. They are super useful for testing UI/UX design, Pack Testing, and call-to-action visibility.

2. Wearable Eye-Tracking Glasses

These lightweight spectacles are equipped with tiny cameras and sensors. They are perfect for in-store research, shelf studies, or real-world navigation. You can see exactly how people shop in a store, not in theory but in practice.

3. Remote Eye Trackers

These sit at a distance and use infrared and camera systems to track gaze without requiring users to wear or touch anything. Great for testing TV ads, key Visuals, Pack Designs, or for that matter, any content which can be put on a screen while keeping participants comfortable.

4. VR-Based Eye Trackers

Built into virtual reality headsets, these analyze gaze within immersive environments. Ideal for testing store layouts, in-game ad placements, or even virtual product showcases.

5. Smart Device Integration

Some smart TVs, monitors, and even mobile devices now have built-in eye-tracking. This enables passive, real-world tracking as consumers engage with content in their natural environment, such as binge-watching on the couch.

How Does Eye-Tracking Actually Work?

The science is pretty cool, yet at the base level, it is incredibly simple

1. Infrared Light: The device emits invisible infrared light toward your eyes.

2. Corneal Reflection: The light reflects off your cornea (the eye's outer layer).

3. Sensor Capture: Cameras detect this reflection and calculate the precise angle of your gaze.

4. Software Analysis: Algorithms translate all that into visual data, showing where you looked, for how long, and in what sequence.

It's like GPS for your eyes.

What Does Eye-Tracking Reveal?

Here are the key outputs that marketers absolutely love:

- **Fixations**

These are the moments when your eyes stop and absorb visual information, usually 100–200 milliseconds or more. Longer fixations mean deeper attention.

Example: If someone's eyes fixate on a product benefit on a pack, they actually read it, not just skim past it.

- **Saccades**

These are rapid eye movements between fixations. You're not taking in data here—you're just scanning. Studying saccades tells you how the eyes travel across a visual scene.

Example: In a web ad, do users jump from the headline to the CTA, or skip the message entirely?

- **Gaze Path**

This maps the sequence of fixations and saccades—essentially the journey your eyes take. Marketers use this to optimize layout and information flow.

Example: If users read the logo, then the footer, then circle back, something's off with the content hierarchy.

- **Heatmaps**

Probably the most popular visual output—these show "hot" areas of attention in red and "cold" zones in blue. You can instantly see what got attention and what didn't.

Example: If 80% of the attention on your pack is going to the top, where your logo sits, but not the bottom, where key benefits are listed, you've got a problem.

Applications of Eye-Tracking in Marketing

Now that you know *how* it works, let's talk about where it shines:

1. Ad Testing: Measure which elements of your ad grab attention, and which get ignored. Headlines, visuals, logos, product shots... it's all trackable.

Example: An automotive brand finds that people love the car photo but skip the promo text. They reposition it closer to the image. The result? Higher recall.

2. Packaging & Shelf Testing: In-store attention is brutally competitive. Eye-tracking shows[9] whether your product stands out—and where on the pack consumers actually look.

Example: A beverage company tests three labels. One version gets noticed faster because of its high contrast and central logo placement, so it launches that one.

3. Website and App Optimization: Track how users navigate your digital platform. Where do they get stuck? What do they ignore? What's slowing them down?

Example: An e-commerce brand finds users missing the "Buy Now" button. After changing its color and position, conversions go up 12%.

4. Print and Email Campaigns: Find out which part of your brochure or email gets read, and where people drop off.

Example: A real estate flyer hides pricing in a dense paragraph. Eye-tracking reveals it's ignored. A redesign with bold pricing boosts inquiries.

5. Product Interaction: Track how people use your product for the first time. Where do they look? What confuses them?

Example: A kitchen appliance maker learns that users can't find the power button. They move it, and satisfaction scores improve.

6. Retail & Store Layout: Observe shopper gaze in real or simulated environments. Are they noticing signage? Promotions? How do they navigate the store?

Example: A cosmetics chain uses eye-tracking glasses in-store.

Data shows customers miss the promotional stand near the entrance. The layout is adjusted, and footfall increases.

Why Eye-Tracking Matters

In marketing, you can't afford to guess where someone is looking. Every second of visual attention is precious real estate. With eye-tracking, you can:

- See what truly gets noticed
- Understand how visual attention flows
- Eliminate blind spots in design
- Back up creative decisions with hard data

And when you pair it with tools like EEG, you don't just know *where* people looked—you also know *how they felt* about what they saw. That's when marketing moves from art... to science.

25

FACIAL CODING

"Sometimes, the face says it all—long before the words catch up."

Picture this: you're in school, final year project in hand, walking carefully to your desk. Just as you sit down, your best friend Mia bumps into your table. Bam! Your project tumbles and shatters. Total disaster. She doesn't say a word at first, but her face? Her eyebrows shoot up in panic, lips pressed, eyes wide with guilt. And though she mouths a small "sorry," she really doesn't need to. You already *knew* how she felt.

That's the magic of facial expressions. They're honest, instant, and universal. The human face is one of the most powerful emotional billboards ever made.

In fact, our face reacts milliseconds before our brain fully processes what we're feeling. So when someone sees an ad, a product, or a brand logo, their facial muscles often betray their feelings—whether they like it, hate it, or feel absolutely nothing.

And this is exactly what facial coding is built on.

What Is Facial Coding?

Facial coding is a method of decoding people's emotional responses based on their facial expressions. It's a tool marketers use to figure out how people feel—consciously or subconsciously—when encountering a brand, ad, or product.

We might *say* "Yeah, it's nice" in a survey. But the face can quietly say "bored" or "confused" or "delighted," depending on micro-movements we're often unaware of.

And that's what makes facial coding so powerful. It's honest. It's fast. And unlike focus groups or surveys, it doesn't lie.

The Science Behind the Smile

At the heart of facial coding lies a fascinating system called the Facial Action Coding System (FACS), created by psychologist Paul Ekman. This framework breaks down facial expressions into Action Units (AUs), which are individual muscle movements on your face.

Each emotion is made up of a combination of these AUs.

Here's a quick cheat sheet:

Action Unit	Movement	Emotion
AU12	Lip corner puller	Happiness (Smiling)
AU1	Inner brow raiser	Sadness or concern
AU4	Brow lowerer	Anger or focus
AU5	Upper eyelid raiser	Surprise or fear
AU9	Nose wrinkler	Disgust
AU14	Dimpler (side smirk)	Contempt or smugness

These combinations form the facial expressions we see every day, but rarely decode consciously.

The Seven Universal Emotions

Across every culture—yes, even the most remote village—people express these seven core emotions in the same way:

1. Happiness – Cheeks raised, eyes crinkled, lips upturned
2. Surprise – Wide eyes, raised brows, mouth open

3. Sadness – Brows pulled inward, drooping mouth corners
4. Anger – Eyebrows drawn down, tight lips
5. Fear – Eyebrows raised and together, eyes wide, lips stretched
6. Disgust – Nose wrinkled, upper lip raised
7. Contempt – One side of the mouth raised in a smirk

These aren't cultural. They're biological. Hardwired into us.

How Facial Coding Works in Marketing

Marketing is emotional. Always has been. Always will be. Facial coding gives you a front-row seat to the emotions your campaign triggers—without asking a single question. It reveals the truth behind the smile, the hesitation behind the nod, and the disconnect hidden beneath politeness. Used thoughtfully, it's not just about measuring reactions—it's about designing for emotional resonance.

Modern facial coding tools use webcams, smartphone cameras, or built-in sensors to read tiny muscle movements. Advanced software, often powered by AI and computer vision, then maps these to emotional states—live, in real time.

So imagine this:

Someone is watching a video ad. The system tracks their expressions second by second, noting the precise moment they smile, frown, furrow their brow, or go completely blank.

For marketers, this is gold. It lets them pinpoint:
- What parts of an ad make people happy
- When confusion creeps in
- Which scenes spark emotion
- And when people emotionally disconnect

Why It's Valuable
- It's unfiltered. People can fake words, but not micro-expressions.
- It works across cultures (with some limitations, which we will discuss later). A smile in Delhi is the same as a smile in Denmark.

- It's silent. You can track emotion without needing people to speak at all.
- It's moment-by-moment. Unlike a survey that says "I liked it," this shows exactly *when* they liked it—or didn't.

Applications in Marketing

Let's bring this down to the real world. Here's how brands use facial coding:

1. Ad Testing: Facial coding helps identify emotional highs and lows during a commercial. Did that heartfelt scene land? Did the humor fall flat?

Example: A chocolate brand's ad shows a child hugging their parent. Facial coding shows joy spikes at that moment, but confusion at the end when the product is rushed in. They revised the ending for better clarity.

2. Product Testing: First impressions matter. Facial coding catches the immediate emotional reaction when someone tastes, touches, or sees a product for the first time.

Example: A beverage brand tests a new drink. Surveys say "It's okay," but facial coding catches brief micro-expressions of disgust during the first sip. Time to rethink the formula—or the positioning.

3. Packaging Design: Packaging is the first point of contact. Does it trigger curiosity? Excitement? Or is it forgettable?

Example: A skincare brand tests two package designs. One sparks joy and interest; the other gets a subtle frown. The winning pack boosts brand recall significantly.

4. UX/UI and Digital Journeys: Whether it's a website or app, facial coding can track emotional flow across the experience.

Example: An e-commerce platform tracks facial expressions during checkout. A spike in confusion reveals a design flaw—quick fix, fewer cart drop-offs.

Outputs You Get from Facial Coding
- Emotion Graphs: Show how the intensity of emotions changes over time
- Emotional Heatmaps: Visuals that highlight which parts of a page or video evoke stronger emotional reactions

Together, these tools help marketers craft emotionally intelligent campaigns that connect, rather than just communicate.

Limitations of Current Facial Coding Algorithms

Facial coding isn't perfect. Like any tool, it comes with limitations, especially across different cultures.

Let's break a few of them down:

1. Cultural Display Rules: In some cultures, people express emotions openly (like the US). In other countries (like Japan), people are taught to mask their feelings for social harmony. A smile might mean joy or just politeness.

2. Expression Frequency: In high-context cultures, people use more subtle, nonverbal expressions, while in others, they are more overt. This can affect algorithm accuracy.

3. Bias in Training Data: Most facial coding software has been trained on Western faces, often male and white. This can lead to misclassification of emotions in people from underrepresented ethnic backgrounds.

4. Anatomy and Physiology Differences: Facial muscle structure varies across ethnicities. Thinner muscles, subtle folds—these differences can trip up even the best algorithms.

How Do We Solve This?
- Train algorithms on diverse, multicultural datasets
- Involve local experts for context-aware interpretation
- Design AI that understands context, not just facial geometry. Only then can facial coding truly become universal.

26

IMPLICIT ASSOCIATION TESTING[7] (IAT)

"What we say we believe... and what we actually believe? Sometimes, they're miles apart."

Let me tell you a little story. A major automobile brand—think luxury meets innovation—was gearing up to launch its first fully electric SUV. Now, this wasn't just another car; this was their leap into the future. So naturally, they ran focus groups.

They asked the usual questions:
"Do you care about sustainability?"
"Would you consider buying an EV?"
"Do you think green technology is important?"
And guess what? People nodded. Smiled. Said all the right things. "Of course I support sustainability!" "I'd love to drive an electric vehicle."

The brand took those answers and ran with them—literally. Their entire ad campaign screamed *eco-friendly*: lush forests, clean air, glowing sunsets, kids playing with butterflies. They painted the dream.

And yet...Sales were flat. Buzz was low. People weren't excited.

Confused, they dug deeper. This time, they ran something different—an Implicit Association Test[7] (IAT).

What they discovered shook them.

While people said they supported green tech, the IAT showed that deep down, many still associated "electric" with "slow," "fragile," and—this one hurt—"uncool." The subconscious said, especially among young male drivers, "EVs aren't sexy."

Armed with this insight, the brand pivoted. The next campaign dropped the trees and nature and focused on torque, speed, and sleek design. The new message? *Electric is powerful. Electric is badass.* And guess what? The car flew off the lot.

What is IAT, really?

Implicit Association Testing[7] is a psychological technique used to measure the strength of subconscious associations in our minds. It reveals what people feel about a brand, product, or concept—even if they don't know it themselves.

Think of it this way: our brains are filled with quick-fire mental links. Apple = Innovation. Volvo = Safety. Some are positive, some are outdated, and some are deeply buried.

IAT uncovers these. Unlike surveys, where we think and respond, IAT focuses on speed. It measures how quickly we associate concepts like "Brand X" with "trustworthy," "luxury," or even "boring."

The faster the response, the stronger the mental connection. That's what makes it so powerful—it bypasses filters, fear of judgment, and social correctness.

How IAT Works

Here's the gist: Participants sit down in front of a computer or mobile screen. They're shown words or images—brand logos, product names, adjectives like "cheap" or "innovative"—in quick succession.

They're asked to sort them into groups by pressing keys. One key might be for "Luxury" and another for "Budget." The test subtly switches combinations to mix and match brands with different attributes.

And here's the trick: if it takes longer to associate your brand with "Luxury" than "Cheap," well... that says something.

Speed = truth. Delay = doubt.

Every millisecond is a clue to what's really going on beneath the surface.

Why IAT Is a Game-Changer in Marketing

Let's be honest. People don't always say what they mean.

Sometimes they don't *know* what they mean. Other times, they want to look good. Or maybe they're in a group and don't want to stand out.

This is where IAT shines. It's:

- Non-verbal – no awkward questions, just fast reactions
- Unfiltered – no time to lie or overthink
- Scalable – easy to administer online
- Predictive – strong subconscious links often predict real-world behavior

In short, IAT is your truth serum.

Applications of IAT in Marketing

Let's explore where IAT adds real value:

1. Brand Perception & Image

How do consumers *really* feel about your brand? You might think they see you as "premium" or "reliable." But do their subconscious minds agree?

Example: A luxury car brand uses IAT to test whether customers associate their name with "status" or "performance." Surprisingly, the link to "performance" is weak. It's time for a messaging realignment.

2. Ad Campaign Impact

Did your campaign land the way you hoped? Traditional tools can't always tell. But IAT can reveal if it truly shifted perceptions.

Example: A skincare brand launches a new anti-aging cream with ads focused on "youthful radiance." Post-campaign IAT shows stronger subconscious links to "beauty" and "confidence"—mission accomplished.

3. Packaging & Product Design

Want to know if your new packaging screams "modern" or "cheap"? Ask the brain, not the mouth.

Example: A beverage company redesigns its label to feel more sophisticated. IAT confirms faster associations with "premium" and "refreshing." Success.

4. Uncovering Consumer Biases

This one's tricky—but important. IAT can reveal implicit stereotypes or biases that might affect how your product is perceived.

Example: A sportswear brand tests how consumers associate certain colors or designs with gender. Results show that some items are subconsciously linked to "masculine" or "feminine" despite unisex branding. Insight leads to a more inclusive design strategy.

But Let's Be Real – It's Not a Magic Wand

While IAT is powerful, it's not infallible.

It doesn't tell you *why* someone feels a certain way. And like any test, it needs proper design, validation, and interpretation. Also, context matters—a lot. Misreading IAT data without considering the emotional or cultural landscape can be misleading. But when used alongside traditional methods, it adds a layer of subconscious truth that most surveys simply miss.

Bringing It All Together

Marketing today is no longer just about shouting your message the loudest. It's about whispering directly into the consumer's subconscious, and tools like IAT are indispensable for that.

They help answer the questions that truly matter:
- What do people *really* think about your brand?
- What do they *feel*, without realizing?
- And most importantly: how can you shape those hidden perceptions before they shape you?

PART 9:
HOW "NEUROSENSUM" IS HELPING MARKETERS
Watching Neuroscience-based Research in Action

27

THE EVOLUTION OF NEUROSCIENCE AND AI-BASED MARKETING RESEARCH

If you've ever sat through a focus group or analyzed a customer survey, you know the drill. People will tell you what they *think* they feel. Or what they *think* you want to hear. But somewhere, deep down, you know there's more to the story. Something that lies beneath the surface of words.

This has been the reality of marketing research for decades, especially in the fast-paced world of FMCG. We've relied heavily on interviews, surveys, and good old group discussions to decode what consumers want. These methods gave us decent insights, sure, but they scratched only the surface. They rarely touched the unconscious layer that quietly influences *real* buying decisions.

But then the game began to change.

The term "**NeuroMarketing**" entered the scene sometime in the early 2000s.

A Dutch researcher named Ale Smidts coined it in 2002, and from there, the world of marketing took a sharp turn into the brain. Suddenly, we were no longer just listening to what consumers *said*—we were watching what their *brains* did.

Brands began experimenting with tools like EEG (electroencephalography) and fMRI (functional MRI). It sounds high-tech—and it is. But in essence, these tools allowed marketers to see how the brain reacted when someone saw a product pack, watched a TV ad, or browsed a store shelf—no more guesswork. If someone paid more for a pasta pack with *less* pasta and *less* sauce, we could finally ask: Why?

That's when companies like NeuroFocus and EmSense came in with a fresh value proposition: let's not just analyse consumer opinions—let's decode their subconscious. And for FMCG brands, this was gold. Because let's face it, in this space, everything happens fast. Product cycles are short, competition is brutal, and consumer loyalty is fragile.

But there was a catch. These early neuro-tools were bulky, expensive, and mostly lab-bound. Not the most scalable, especially in markets like ours where agility matters.

The real breakthrough came in the mid-2010s when AI entered the picture.

Now this was different. Suddenly, marketers could sift through mountains of unstructured data—social media chatter, videos, consumer rants—at breakneck speed. AI-powered tools could now do predictive modelling, sentiment analysis, and even real-time idea testing. What took weeks earlier now takes minutes.

But here's the best part—AI didn't push neuroscience out. Instead, it *partnered* with it, like two puzzle pieces finally fitting together.

By the late 2010s, we started seeing some incredible things. Platforms like **Neurosensum Technology**, Neurons Inc., and Realeyes began combining EEG, Eye Tracking, facial coding, biometrics, and AI into seamless, scalable solutions. No longer were we tied to the lab.

We could test how someone's brain and body responded to an ad, a pack, or a shelf placement—anywhere, anytime.

Thanks to advances in computer vision and deep learning, Emotion AI took things to a whole new level. Imagine testing facial expressions using a simple webcam and gaining culturally nuanced insights, whether you're in Jakarta or Johannesburg. That's exactly what companies like Affectiva started offering.

Now, as someone in the trenches, I can tell you—**Neurosensum** played a big role in making all this practical. We worked hard to reduce EEG testing costs, making it accessible beyond just big brands. And we didn't stop there. We developed the NeuroEquity Model, built smartly around Implicit Association Test[7]ing (IAT), which helps brands map their subconscious strengths and weaknesses with surgical precision. And lately, we have also developed Product Test using EEG, which would be a game changer for R&D teams as they can really go beyond the rationalized responses and can develop products which are truly appealing to the consumer's palette.

Today, as we edge further into this decade, marketing research is no longer just about "big data"—it's about "deep data." We're seeing a world of hyper-personalization, instant feedback loops, and growing ethical consciousness. Brands are now fine-tuning the colour of their pack, the beat of their sonic logo, and even the emotional crescendo of their TV ad—all based on hard neuroscience.

And that, to me, is the heart of this evolution. We're no longer asking, *"What do people say?"* We ask, *"What do they feel—even if they can't put it into words?"*

It's a shift—not just in methods but in mindset—from listening to the surface noise to truly understanding the quiet signals the brain sends.

Welcome to the era where your consumer's brain is your best focus group.

28

NEUROSCIENCE AND AI-BASED MARKETING RESEARCH TO IMPROVE THE 6PS

Alright, so we've spoken about how neuroscience and AI are shaking up the world of marketing research. But now comes the big question—how do we use all this science actually to improve marketing decisions on the ground? Especially across the good old 6Ps—Product, Price, Place, Promotion, People, and Process?

Let me share a perspective that's close to my heart, because I've lived this journey from the inside. As the Co-founder and Managing Director of Neurosensum, this isn't just theory for me. It's what we breathe and build every day. When we started Neurosensum, our goal was clear: we didn't want to be just another tech company throwing jargon at marketers. We wanted to make *science usable*. Something that could plug directly into real business decisions—quickly, affordably, and with clarity.

That's where our approach stands out. We combine neuroscience, AI, and behavioral science to provide brands with deep and actionable insights. Not months later. But in the moment when it matters.

To further improve the process, we developed SurveySensum, which brings in the AI magic. SurverSensum is a super agile Customer Experience (CX) platform that listens to customers in real time—from surveys, chats, social media rants, app reviews—you name it. The system makes sense of all this chaos and gives you sharp, structured insights. We are further improving SurveySensum to make it like an end-to-end solution for the client where the client just needs to give a few prompts to get things done.

So, what happens when you combine Neurosensum's deep neuro tools with SurveySensum's AI engine? You get a 360-degree powerhouse. A full-stack system that understands *what the brain feels, what the eyes notice, what the fingers type,* and *what the customer actually says.*

Let's look at how we apply this to each of the 6Ps. Just glance at this little table below—it breaks it all down:

Marketing Aspect	NeuroSensum Products
Brand	*NS NeuroEquityFunnel*
	NS NeuroImage
Product	*NS MyndSensory*
Promotion (Ads)	*NS MyndSight,*
	NS MyndTune
Packaging	*NS PackSense*
Pricing	*NS NeuroImage*
Place (Shopper Exp)	*NS ShopperSense*
People & Process	*SurveySensum Text Analytics*

Each of these tools is designed to collect data, decode emotions, track attention, and capture real-time customer intent.

Whether you're crafting a new ad, refining a product's taste, testing the effectiveness of your pack design, or trying to understand why service complaints keep popping up, there's a neuroscience or AI-powered lens that can help you see clearly.

And that's the beauty of this approach—it's not about replacing human intuition. It's about *supporting it with science*. This gives brand leaders, marketers, researchers, and designers a window into what the consumer doesn't always say but deeply *feels*.

Because at the end of the day, isn't that what all great marketing is about? Knowing your customer so well that you can anticipate their needs, align with their emotions, and serve them in a way that feels effortless.

We'll dive into each of these tools in detail next, starting with how we decode ad engagement using EEG. But before we go there, just pause and think: If you could see what your consumer's brain and body go through when they see your product, hear your jingle, or hold your packaging in their hand, what would you change?

Turns out, now you *can*.

Awesome. Let's now bring Neurosensum MyndSight, the EEG-based solution for ad testing, to life. We'll keep that same natural, human tone, with a hint of curiosity, practicality, and grounded storytelling.

A
NEUROSENSUM MYNDSIGHT
Listening to the Brain During Your Ads

Let's admit it: every marketer loves the ads they produce. It's their baby. After all, it's got the emotional storyline, the perfect shot, maybe even a catchy jingle. But here's the million-dollar question: Does your audience love it too? And more importantly, do their brains?

Because liking something *consciously* and reacting to it *subconsciously* are two entirely different things.

That's where Neurosensum MyndSight steps in. This EEG-based ad testing platform is designed to decode what consumers feel while watching your ad, not after. This isn't about "How did you like it?" It's about, "What was your brain doing when that scene played?"

And why is this important?. Because when someone is watching an ad and feels that it is boring, they will switch the channel or move their attention to another screen in their hand, or even wander into their thoughts. There would be no one there to force her to see the ad till the end and decide her liking.

So, how does it work?

So, imagine this: Your ad (whether it's a sleek TV commercial, a quirky Instagram reel, or even a rough storyboard) is shown to a respondent. But we don't show it in isolation. We drop it in a sea of clutter, just like the viewer would experience in the real world.

After all, that's how people see your ad—sandwiched between the real content and other ads.

While the participant watches, they wear a lightweight EEG headset. At the same time, an eye-tracking system silently records where they're looking. These two tools work like a duet—the EEG catches what's happening inside the brain (attention, emotion, mental effort), while the eye-tracker maps where the eyes go. The magic happens when we fuse this data using our in-house algorithm. What we get is a second-by-second "brain state map" of how the viewer *truly* experiences the ad.

What kind of content can be tested?

This isn't just for polished, final videos. Any format can be tested, such as animatics, stills, or even a rough storyboard. In fact, testing at these early stages is a blessing—if something's not working (maybe a confusing plot point or an emotionless scene), we catch it *before* you sink money into production.

So yes, you save budget, time, and your brand from airing an ad that doesn't land.

What are we measuring?

We focus on two primary EEG metrics:

- **Relaxation Score** – How calm and mentally open is the viewer? It reflects emotional ease and receptivity.
- **Attention Score** – How focused is the viewer at any given moment? Are they dialed in or zoning out?

Based on these, we create four emotional brain states:

- **Engaged** (High Attention, High Relaxation): Jackpot. They're loving it.
- **Bored** (Low Attention, High Relaxation): They're chill... but not in a good way.
- **Puzzled** (High Attention, Low Relaxation): Something's off—they're trying to figure it out.
- **Snoozing** (Low Attention, Low Relaxation): Ouch. You've lost them.
- **Moderate** – This brain state is a moment that is not very clear, and the consumer's brain is transitioning between one brain state and another.

These brain states are then compared with **normative data**, so you're not just seeing how your ad did *in isolation*, but how it stacks up against what's typical for your category or region.

So, why should a marketer care?

In today's world, people are bombarded with content. Attention spans are shorter than ever. And unfortunately, we're often just guessing which version of an ad works best.

But with EEG insights, you get solid, brain-backed answers to key creative questions:

- **Where does the advertisement lose impact?** – We pinpoint the exact moment when attention dwindles or emotions fade.
- **Which version is more effective?** – If you're torn between two edits, we reveal which one resonates better in the brain.
- **Are emotions aligned with your message?** – If your goal is to inspire, but the EEG indicates annoyance or confusion, that's a warning sign.
- **Will it be memorable?** – Advertisements that evoke strong emotional reactions are more likely to be remembered. That's your initial step toward recall and conversion.
- **Which are the winning moments?** – Understanding this helps in developing stronger, smaller edits of the ad and also knowing which scenes of the ad to dial up more in the campaign through other media (example, Instagram reels).

In essence, MyndSight lets you go beyond guesswork. It helps you shape ads that don't just "look good" or "sound cool" but actually connect, engage, and convert—the kind of ads that linger in memory long after the screen goes dark.

B
NEUROSENSUM MYNDSENSORY
What Your Brain Tastes Before You Speak

Let's talk about something we all love—food. Or maybe a fragrant shampoo. Or that irresistible crunch of a new snack. Now think about it—how do we *really* experience a product? It's not just taste or smell. It's a full-on sensory journey, often playing out in micro-moments we're unaware of.

And that's where MyndSensory steps in. This isn't your average product test where someone says, "I like it," or "It's okay." This is neuroscience going right to the source—to the brain—and asking: *What are you actually feeling right now, even if you can't put it into words?* Because let's face it, consumers often struggle to explain *why* they like a product. And traditional surveys can't pick up the nuances of aroma, texture, or aftertaste. But the brain? It responds instantly. Silently. Honestly.

So, what is MyndSensory?

It's an EEG-based platform we've built at Neurosensum to decode subconscious responses to a product, stage by stage. Think of it like watching someone's inner movie while they experience a product in real time. We track the brain's every reaction from first glance to final aftertaste.

Here's how it works:

We lead consumers through a guided sensory ritual. It's not just "try this." It's structured, time-controlled exposure to stages like:

- Appearance
- Aroma
- Taste
- Aftertaste

Each stage is timed—usually around 10 to 20 seconds—so the brain gets just enough time to process the stimulus, and we can capture a clean, distinct signal.

Participants wear an EEG headset, of course. But this process is powerful because we also sync the sensory steps with a custom-built mobile app. The app guides the flow while syncing each moment with brainwave recordings. So if someone flinches at the aftertaste or lights up at the aroma, we know exactly when and why.

It's not just a brain scan—it's a live, sensory diary.

What are we measuring?

Two big scores drive this system:

- **Familiarity Score** – Does this product feel familiar or comforting? Does it align with what they've experienced before?
- **Engagement Score** – How emotionally or cognitively involved are they? Are they loving it Or Not?

We use these two axes to map each product into one of five distinct "brain states":

- **Delightful** (High Familiarity + High Engagement): The dream zone. Recognized, loved, and emotionally satisfying.
- **Novel** (Low Familiarity + High Engagement): Intriguing and new—could be a winner if positioned right.
- **Basic** (High Familiarity + Low Engagement): Feels known, but meh. Safe but not exciting.
- **Neutral** (Middle of the road): Neither here nor there. Usually, it's a sign that something's missing.
- **Rejected** (Low Familiarity + Low Engagement): Uh-oh. This isn't connecting at all.

This framework gives you a roadmap—whether to launch, refine, reposition, or rethink.

However, this methodology is only relevant for sensory categories which is impacted by any of our senses – Smell, Taste, or even Touch to some extent.

These would be largely Food, Beverages, and even cosmetic categories where Perfume plays an important role in selection.

Where does this help businesses?

Now, this is where things get real. Let's say you're testing a new chocolate variant, a health drink, or a beauty product. Traditional taste tests will give you opinions, but MyndSensory gives you *neural truth*.

- **Choosing between prototypes** – Which product version lights up the brain? EEG reveals the winner, even before consumers verbalize it.
- **Fine-tuning sensory elements**—Maybe the issue is not the whole product, it's the aftertaste or the texture. MyndSensory pinpoints where the drop-off happens. Especially when conscious ratings are combined with individual consumer-level subconscious scores.
- **Comparison with competition** – You can go head-to-head with a rival product and see who wins the brain's affection.
- **Validating innovation** – Is your new idea exciting or just confusing? This tool tells you how the brain reacts to novelty, long before you go to market.

And here's the big advantage: EEG doesn't just measure *what* someone says—they might be polite or unsure—it measures *how* their brain reacts, silently and immediately.

So the next time you're launching a new product, don't just ask, "Do you like it?"

Ask instead: Did your brain love it, *even before you knew you did?*

C
NEUROSENSUM MYNDTUNE
What Does Your Brand Sound Like in the Brain?

Close your eyes for a second.

Now imagine the Netflix "ta-dum." Or that tiny Nokia ringtone from the early 2000s. Or Britannia's "ting-ting-ting-ting..." Or if you are in Indonesia the "To-ko-Pedia" tune

Did you hear it?

That's the power of sonic branding.

Music, jingles, sonic logos—these aren't just add-ons anymore. They're emotional shortcuts. Within a fraction of a second, the right tune can spark recognition, bring back memories, or even create desire. The right sound can lodge your brand into a consumer's subconscious faster than any visual. But here's the challenge—how do you *know* if your brand's sound is actually doing that? Is it calming or irritating? Memorable or forgettable? Emotional or flat?

That's where MyndTune comes in.

It's our neuroscience-driven, EEG-based testing platform that tells you exactly how your brand's music lands—not on Spotify, but inside the brain.

So, what is MyndTune?

At its heart, MyndTune helps brands evaluate the subconscious, emotional reaction to their audio assets—whether it's a full jingle, a sonic logo, or a musical tagline. We combine EEG brainwave mapping with traditional feedback and AI-based analysis to get a complete emotional and cognitive profile of your sonic branding.

Because music isn't just heard. It's *felt*.

How does it work?

It's a beautifully layered process:

1. We recruit respondents from your target audience—real people who use (or could use) your brand.

2. In a controlled setting, we set them up with EEG headsets and play different sonic assets—this could be a full-length track, instrumental versions, or even a few variations of the same jingle.

3. While they listen, we track their brainwave patterns, capturing subconscious reactions second by second.

4. After that, we collect conscious feedback through a short survey, asking about emotional tone, brand fit, clarity, etc.

This dual-method approach gives us both the *heartbeats* and the *headspace* of the consumer experience.

What do we measure?

With EEG, we break down brain activity across six different bands (like Delta, Theta, Alpha, etc.), then map that into clear emotional states. Here are some of the outputs:

- **Enjoyment Score** – Is the music pleasant? Does the brain *like* it?
- **Relaxation Score** – Is it calming? Or does it create tension?

Based on these two core measures, we create Brain states, which we can interpret second by second of Sonic Stimulus.

Brain State Classification – We categorize listener responses into:

- Pleasant & Enjoyable
- Curious & Exciting
- Boring & Dull
- Annoying & Irritating
- Emotionally Neutral

What does it solve for your brand?

Think about this: Your consumer might see your pack once a week. But they might *hear* your jingle multiple times a day—on TV, on YouTube, in a store, or a notification on the app.

Sound cuts deeper, faster. You can close your Eyes, but your ears remain open and listen to everything around you.

Here's how MyndTune helps:

- **Strengthen sensory identity** – Match your audio with your brand's core emotions: joy, trust, care, excitement.
- **Stand out in the clutter** – A memorable sound can be your anchor in a noisy media world.
- **Refine sonic assets** – Don't just go with what "sounds nice." Go with what *feels right in the brain*.
- **Segment-based optimization** – Want to know if kids or moms prefer a tune? We'll break it down for you.
- **Reduce subjectivity** – Take the guesswork out of audio feedback. This is not "my boss liked this version." It's "the consumer's brain preferred it."

Because let's face it—your sound strategy is only as strong as the *emotion* it triggers. With MyndTune, we help you compose not just music but also memory.

D
NEUROSENSUM PACKSENSE
Making Packaging That the Eyes Can't Ignore

Let's be honest—packaging is your silent salesperson. It's what your customer sees before they hear your jingle or read your tagline. In a retail store, that split-second glance at a shelf? That's your first impression. And we all know—you never get a second chance at that.

But here's the tricky part: shelves are crowded. Everyone's shouting for attention. And consumers?

They don't scan each product like a robot—they *skim*. They glance, they pause, they move on. So, the real question is—*are their eyes even stopping on your pack?*

That's exactly what PackSense is built to answer. It's our flagship eye-tracking-based solution, which helps brands understand how their packaging actually performs in the chaos of a real or simulated shelf. There is no guesswork—just raw, eye-level truth.

How does PackSense work?

We approach this in two steps, exactly how consumers experience it. First, how do they see the pack on the shelf (we call it Zoom out Evaluation), and then how they look at it from close proximity, looking at different elements of the pack (which we call Zoom in evaluation). Let's understand each of these in detail.

1. Zoom Out Evaluation – Shelf Test with Portable Eye-Tracking Glasses

This is as close to real life as it gets. We take your consumers, ask them to browse a real or virtual shelf while wearing lightweight,

wearable eye-tracking glasses. As they walk through the store, the glasses silently record everything:
- What pack catches their eye first
- How long do they look at each pack
- Where they glance, linger, and skip
- Which part of the shelf is most visible, and which is a blind spot

In all, this tells us how your product performs *on the shelf.* Does it stand out? Or does it get swallowed by the visual clutter?

For Zoom-out evaluation, we can evaluate Real Shelf with real products or a Printed Shelf (in case the stimulus is not available), or even on a large screen if time or budget is a constraint.

2. Zoom In Evaluation – Static Screen Testing for Deep Dive

Here, we use a screen-based eye tracker and show the consumer looking at a still image or a digital mockup of your pack.

This setup is perfect when you want to dissect the design—determine whether your logo is being seen, whether claims are noticed, and whether the layout flows the way you intended.

Together, these two methods provide a comprehensive 360-degree view of how your pack performs on the shelf *and* how its elements communicate up close.

What do we measure?

Let's look at some key visual metrics that PackSense captures:
- **% Respondent Seen**—How many consumers noticed your pack or key element? If your brand name or callout isn't getting seen, you're losing that first battle.
- **Time to First Notice**—How quickly does someone spot your pack? A lower number here means a better shelf standout.
- **Share of Time Spent**—How long do their eyes stay after seeing your pack? A higher number = more engagement and interest.

- **Share of Facings Index**—This one's clever. It tells you whether your pack is getting *more* or *less* attention than it should, based on its physical space on the shelf.
- **Heatmaps**—You can even generate heat maps that visually show where consumers are looking—and more importantly, where they aren't.

For Zoom in Evaluation, we can evaluate Pictures (2D, 3D) and even real mockups.

Many more analytical frameworks help us answer different marketing questions.

So, what are the marketing questions we can answer?

This isn't just design feedback—it's strategy in disguise. Here's how brands use PackSense:

- **Shelf Visibility** – Is your product noticeable from a distance, or does it fade into the background noise? Might need a design revamp
- **Planogram Testing** – Where should your product be placed on the shelf to get the most attention? High? Eye-level? Bottom? We test it all. Obviously, you would need to do a cost-benefit analysis based on the cost incurred to place your product in different parts of the shelves.
- **Pack Browsability** – Once the eyes land, do they flow smoothly through your pack, from the logo to the variant to the benefit? Or are they getting stuck or skipping key info? Do you need to redesign the pack to make the key elements stick out?
- **Design Element Testing** - Is your claim being noticed? Is the logo placed correctly? Are the colors helping or hurting?
- **Differentiation and Clarity** – Can people tell one variant from another? Are they confused between your chocolate and your strawberry variants and think that these are from different companies?

- **A/B Testing** – Got two versions of your design? Let the eyes decide which one works better.

In essence, PackSense helps you make packaging that doesn't just *look* good in the boardroom—it *works* where it matters most: in that split-second decision at the shelf. Because when it comes to packaging, it's not about what you designed. It's about what the consumer sees.

E
NEUROSENSUM SHOPPERSENSE
Getting into the Eyes of the Shopper

Imagine you're standing in a supermarket aisle—let's say, the snack section. Shelves bursting with colour, offers screaming from every corner, and rows of packaging fighting for attention. Now, what does your customer do?

Do they walk straight to your pack? Or glance right past it? Do they spot that standee you worked so hard on? Or are they pulled in by the competition?

This is the kind of behavior ShopperSense helps us decode.

Because here's the truth: shoppers are not rational. They don't always follow the route we assume in our strategy decks. In-store behavior is messy, subconscious, and wildly unpredictable. But if we can *watch* them—quietly, scientifically—we can start to see the patterns. And from those patterns, we get powerful answers.

How does shopper Sense work?

ShopperSense is our portable eye-tracking solution that allows us to follow real shoppers in real retail spaces—not in a lab, not in a simulation, but in the real, chaotic, noisy world of shelves, POSMs and distractions.

Using lightweight eye-tracking glasses, we get a front-row seat to exactly how people navigate a store—what they see, where they pause, what catches their eye, and what they ignore.

It's like walking through the store *with* your customer, but from inside their head.

It's a step-by-step process, and every step adds context:
1. **Recruit real shoppers** – people who actually buy in your category. No hired actors, just authentic consumers.
2. **Natural shopping journey** – There are no prompts or interference. We ask them to shop as usual, and the eye-tracking glasses silently record everything.
3. **Post-shop interviews** – After the journey, we talk to them. We ask why they picked something, what they recall, and how they perceived the overall experience. This gives us the "why" behind the visuals.

What do we actually measure?

Let's break it down:
- **Heat & Route Maps** – Visualize attention zones and foot traffic paths.
- **% Respondent Seen** – Did shoppers even *see* your pack on shelf or special display or your POSM?
- **Time to First Notice** – How long did it take for them to notice any item?
- **Share of Time Spent** – How long did they actually engage with any item?
- **Facings Index** – Are you getting as much attention as your space deserves?

We use all these measures to answer a host of Shopper Marketing Questions?

What kind of business problems can we solve?

Oh, plenty. This is the secret weapon for shopper marketing teams, trade marketers, brand managers, and even sales teams. Here's what we help with:
- Where are your hot spots in-store? Are you in the areas where eyeballs actually go?
- Is your planogram working? Do shoppers browse it intuitively or get lost?
- Are your secondary displays pulling weight? Or just eating on a budget?

HOW "NEUROSENSUM" IS HELPING MARKETERS

- Are POSMs (wobblers, standees, signage) being noticed at all? Which ones we should keep and which ones we can remove?
- Are you aligned with the natural shopper movement? Or swimming against the current?
- How does your display compare with your competitor's? Are you winning attention or leaking it?

The beauty of ShopperSense is that it doesn't just diagnose—it guides. It tells you *what's working, what's not,* and where to intervene.

Because when it comes to retail, you don't win the sale when someone reaches the counter.

You win it in those first few seconds of eye contact, curiosity, and shelf magic.

Lovely—let's keep the rhythm flowing. Now, we're entering the world of brand strategy with Neurosensum's NeuroEquity Funnel—a tool that blends behavioral and emotional data to truly understand how people *feel* about your brand, even when they don't say it out loud.

F
NEUROSENSUM NEUROEQUITY FUNNEL
Seeing Your Brand Strength through the Eyes of the Brain

Let's take a step back for a moment.

You've built a brand. You've invested in ads, packaging, pricing, the works. And maybe you've seen some traction—sales are coming in, awareness seems okay.

But here's the million-rupee question: How strong is your brand in the consumer's mind and heart? Not just in what they tell you, but in how they *feel* about it, deep down?

Because brand equity isn't just a number in a tracker, it's a feeling. A gut instinct. A subconscious memory that drives preference, even when people aren't fully aware of it.

That's why we built the NeuroEquity Funnel—a holistic framework that combines the rational with the emotional, the spoken with the unspoken, the conscious with the subconscious.

So, what's it all about?

At its core, the NeuroEquity Funnel integrates two types of data:

- **System 2 (Conscious Behavioral Data):** This tells us what people *do*—are they aware of your brand? Have they tried it? Are they current users? It's logical, recall-based information.
- **System 1 (Subconscious Emotional Data):** This is the gold. We capture it using Implicit Association Test[7]ing (IAT)—a clever way to measure emotional openness without asking directly.

It works through response time in a gamified setting. The quicker someone selects your brand for future purchase, the stronger the Equity in the Mind (After all, that's what we are building Brand Equity for), and the faster they reject your brand, the weaker the brand is in their mind.

So now, instead of just knowing *who* uses your brand, we also know *how deeply they feel connected to it.*

What does the NeuroEquity funnel look like?

We map people across six emotional-behavioral segments:

1. **Loyal** – Current users with a strong emotional connection. They're your core. Don't just retain them—celebrate them.
2. **Risky** – Also current users, but with low emotional attachment. They're using you, but could switch the moment a rival whispers.
3. **Immediate Potential** – Not using your brand, but emotionally open. With a little nudge, they're ready to try.
4. **Long-Term Potential** – Not using and not yet emotionally engaged. But with storytelling and visibility, they could shift over time. However, these consumers would take some time and effort to target.
5. **Rejectors** – Not interested. Actively closed off. Depending on your resources, you'll need to work hard or not at all.
6. **Unaware** – They've never heard of you. But that's also an opportunity for first impressions done right. And if this is a substantially large segment, this is where you should work first.

Each consumer is classified into one of these buckets. And that's the magic—because now, your brand strategy becomes deeply personal. You're no longer marketing based on their past behavior, but taking into account their Emotional Openness to your brand.

HOW "NEUROSENSUM" IS HELPING MARKETERS

What can you do with this?

We can create a targeting strategy separately for each group of consumers (especially the larger groups) to improve your Overall Brand Performance.

- **Retain Loyalists** – Keep them close. Surprise them. Personalize your messaging. Turn them into brand ambassadors.
- **Convert the Risky** – Understand what's missing emotionally. Is it trust? Is it excitement? Fix it before they leave.
- **Activate the Ready** – The "Immediate Potential" group is a goldmine. With a little push—a free sample, a campaign that hits the right nerve—and boom, you've got new users.
- **Nurture Long-Term Converts** – These folks need time. Don't hard-sell. Tell stories. Build brand presence gently.
- **Understand and maybe let go of Rejectors** – Sometimes, saying, "Not worth the effort is okay." But other times, there's a perception to fix.
- **Grow the Unaware** – This is classic brand-building. Go mass. Go visible. Make your presence felt.

Since each respondent is tagged with a clear profile, you can do deeper dives—understand media habits, campaign responses, barriers to conversion, and decision drivers for *each* segment. It's precise. It's actionable. It's human.

Why is this important?

In today's world, brand building isn't just about shouting louder; it's about knowing who's listening, what they're feeling, and *why*.

The NeuroEquity Funnel helps you move from brand awareness to brand affection—and from there, to brand loyalty. It tells you exactly *where your brand stands*—and even more importantly, where it can go next. Because the truth is, it's not just about how many people know your brand. It's about how many people would *miss it* if it disappeared.

G
NEUROSENSUM NEUROIMAGE
What Your Brand Feels Like in the Subconscious

Let me ask you something simple—what comes to your mind when you hear a brand name like Apple? Or Tata? Or maybe even Maggi?

Without thinking too hard, you'll probably feel something. A vibe. A certain trust, or nostalgia, or maybe excitement.

Now flip that—what do *your consumers* feel when they hear your brand's name? You might think you know. After all, you've done your Brand Tracking surveys and focus groups.

But here's the catch—people are polite. They rationalize. They say things that are safe. Or sometimes, they simply don't know how to articulate what they feel. That's where NeuroImage comes in. It doesn't ask people to describe your brand. It watches how fast their fingers move when their subconscious sees your name.

So, what is NeuroImage and how does it work?

It's a neuroscience-powered method that uses the Implicit Association Test[7] (IAT) to capture emotional perception, not through words, but through reaction time.

It works like this: The respondent sees a series of words or images—some related to your brand, some to specific attributes like "trustworthy," "innovative," "friendly," "expensive," etc. They must tap the screen or hit a key as quickly as possible when they feel the two are linked.

Simple, right?

But here's the beauty—the faster the response, the stronger the subconscious link. It's not about whether they say your brand is premium—it's whether their brain *feels* that association and reacts *automatically*.

All of this happens inside a gamified app—fun, light, and scalable across demographics, geographies, and even languages.

What does it measure?

NeuroImage gives you a set of powerful, emotionally intelligent brand metrics:

- **NeuroImage Score** – A composite score that blends speed, accuracy, and confidence, giving you a single index to track emotional openness toward your brand.
- **Attribute Mapping** – Find out which traits (like "safe," "stylish," "affordable," or "outdated") are strongly or weakly linked to your brand.
- **Competitive Differentiation** – See if your brand owns any emotional territory, or if it's swimming in the same emotional pool as your competitors.

And since it's all digital and scalable, you can slice this data by region, age group, user type—whatever you need for deeper targeting.

What problems does it solve?

This is a marketer's best friend when you need to:

- **Get beyond polite answers** – No more "I think your brand is nice." Now you'll know what they *actually feel*, deep inside.
- **Understand your emotional positioning** – Are you truly perceived as innovative? Or just saying it in your ads while the subconscious says otherwise?
- **Track brand health over time** – Want to see if that expensive campaign actually changed perception? This tool will tell you—not with likes or clicks, but with brain-backed data.

- **Measure the likely impact of a New Concept/Advertisement or a Product launch on the Key Image of your Brand** – by doing a pre-post exposure test
- **Sharpen your communication** – Align your messaging with what consumers already associate with your brand, or use the gaps to reposition.
- **Find your emotional whitespace** – Discover traits that your competitors haven't claimed yet, and build an emotional identity around them.

NeuroImage helps you go from "People say they like us" to "We *know* how they *feel* about us." And in today's hyper-cluttered, emotionally-charged brand world, that's not just a nice-to-have. It is essential knowledge for marketers.

H
SURVEYSENSUM TEXT ANALYTICS (AI)
Hearing What Your Customers Are Really Saying

Let's now move into the final piece of this beautifully interconnected puzzle—SurveySensum Text Analytics. This is where we shift gears a bit.

We're no longer just talking about products or packs, but about the people behind the brand and the processes that shape customer experience.

This part is all about listening—not to the brainwaves or eyeballs—but to the voice of the customer. The angry rants, the subtle compliments, the suggestions no one asked for. Because in the world of service and experience, that's where the gold lies.

Let's be honest—customers have a lot to say.

They type it in chat windows. Leave it in the app store reviews. Blurt it out in call center conversations. Whisper it in open-ended survey comments. And sometimes, they just drop a cryptic one-liner on Twitter.

The challenge isn't that the feedback isn't coming in. The challenge is that it's coming in from everywhere, in different formats, at breakneck speed.

That's where SurveySensum Text Analytics steps in. It's an AI-driven solution that sifts through the chaos and finds meaning. It listens to unstructured feedback and turns it into clear, structured insights—so you know what's working, what's broken, and what needs fixing *right now*.

Because in the service world—be it banks, telecom, e-commerce, healthcare, or hospitality—experience isn't defined by just one interaction. People and Processes shape it.

And when either one fails, the customer *feels* it.

So, what is SurveySensum Text Analytics?

At its core, it's a multilingual, omnichannel feedback analysis engine.

That's a fancy way of saying it reads, tags, interprets, and prioritizes everything your customers say—whether it's typed into a form, said during a support call or tweeted angrily at 2 AM

It uses Natural Language Processing (NLP) and machine learning to analyze feedback across channels like:

- Live chat transcripts
- Social media posts
- App store reviews
- Call center logs
- Survey comments
- Support tickets

And it does this in real time.

How does it work?

Here's the magic behind the curtain:

1. Omnichannel Integration – It pulls data from wherever your customers are talking.
2. Topic Modelling – It automatically groups feedback into themes, like "payment issues," "app crashes," "agent behavior," "long wait times", etc.
3. Sentiment Analysis – It assigns emotion—was this feedback positive, neutral, or negative? And how intense was it?
4. Urgency Detection – High-emotion, critical complaints? It flags and sends them to your team immediately so your team can respond before it becomes a Twitter storm.
5. AI-Generated Summaries – It condenses 10,000 rows of feedback into a simple dashboard, so leadership can take action without drowning in data.
6. And yes, you can query the data using Natural Language Prompts (which is becoming so popular

nowadays) to understand any specific issues that you are trying to understand.
7. And all of this is visualized in interactive dashboards, with drill-down capabilities for teams across departments.

And it works seamlessly in Multiple Languages, making it ideal for cross-market analysis.

Why does this matter for People and Process?

Because in service-led industries, your people *are* your product.

You could have the best digital app, but if your agent sounds rude or your refund process is clunky, the damage is done.

Here's what SurveySensum helps with:

- **Diagnose broken touchpoints** – Before your CSAT tanks or your NPS dips.
- **Improve internal processes** – Find recurring patterns that point to deeper operational flaws.
- **Enable faster issue resolution** – Stop scanning thousands of comments manually, or worse, ignore them because of a lack of resources. Let AI find the red flags instantly.
- **Create a culture of continuous improvement** – Feedback isn't just data—it's your customer whispering, "Here's how you can get better."
- **Build organizational memory** – Don't lose learnings. Over time, let feedback shape training, SOPs, and service design.

In today's world, experience is everything. SurveySensum helps you not just listen but *understand, act,* and *evolve.*

PART 10:
SENSORY BRAND AUDIT
Unleash your Brand's Sensory Memory

29

UNDERSTANDING & USING YOUR BRAND'S SENSORY MEMORY

You know that strange moment when you walk into a store, hear a jingle, catch a whiff of something familiar, and instantly feel like you're back in your childhood? That's not magic—it's sensory memory at play. Now imagine if a brand could consistently trigger that kind of emotional reaction. That's exactly what this framework helps brands do.

The idea is simple yet powerful: uncover, understand, and elevate the sensory memories your brand is already creating, whether you're aware of them or not. And do it with purpose, weaving them into the very fabric of your marketing mix: the 6Ps—Product, Price, Place, Promotion, People, and Process.

This isn't just a feel-good exercise. It's a structured audit that evaluates your sensory footprint and uncovers concrete, actionable ways to enrich how people perceive and remember your brand.

The Grid: Mapping Sensory Memory Across the 6Ps

Let's start with the backbone of this audit—a sensory memory Audit.

For each of the 6 Ps – ask yourself and your consumer – what Kind of Sensory Memory does it have?

For Each Of The 6ps	Brand X Memory
Visual (Vision)	
Sonic (Sound)	
Olfactory (Smell)	
Gustatory (Taste)	
Tactile (Touch)	

This matrix helps you assess how the five senses (Visual, Auditory, Olfactory, Gustatory, and Tactile) are engaged across the 6Ps of marketing.

Step 1: Discovering the Sensory Memories You Already Own

This step is about self-awareness. Before dreaming up new experiences, ask yourself: What do people already associate with our brand deep in their subconscious?

Here's how to find out:

- Run internal workshops. Tap into what your employees, especially frontline teams like marketing and sales, believe the brand feels, smells, and sounds like. Can add the R&D team also to the mix.
- Conduct external research, such as in-depth interviews, sensory recall exercises, or ethnographic studies (yes, the kind where researchers hang out in people's lives).

Ask simple but powerful questions:

- What sensory memories come to mind when customers think of us? Taste, Smell, Texture, Sound, Visuals
- Probe it by each of the 6Ps to get a more specific Answer
- Do the same for competition as well.

You can use tools like:
- Sensory recall boards (think Pinterest, but for brand memories)
- Stimulus response —let people react to packaging textures, sound clips, or color schemes
- Customer journey maps, layered with sensory data

Capture all your findings in the audit grid. That becomes your brand's sensory mirror.

This will help to create an inventory of Sensory Memory across Brands, and you can directly compare if some things are owned only by you and which ones are shared.

Step 2: Interpreting the Story Behind the Senses

Now that you've got the data, it's time to make sense of it. Literally.

Ask yourself:
- Do these sensory cues truly reflect our brand values and positioning?
- Are we evoking the right emotional responses—trust, excitement, nostalgia?
- Are there sensory red flags—unpleasant sounds, jarring visuals, materials that feel cheap?

Also, think deeper:
- What do these cues say about customers' perception of our price point or product quality?
- Are we sending unintentional messages?
- And of course, how are competitors doing in this space? Are they using sensory triggers more cleverly?

This isn't just a diagnosis—it's storytelling. It's about decoding the signals your brand is sending, often without saying a word.

Step 3: Designing the Sensory Future of Your Brand

Here's where it gets exciting. With all these insights, you can fine-tune or reimagine your sensory identity.

Let's break it down by sense:
- **Visual:** Update the logo, color palette, packaging, or even your digital UI. Everything people see matters.

- **Auditory**: Think beyond jingles. Introduce sonic branding, tweak your tone of voice, or train customer service reps to speak more on-brand.
- **Olfactory**: Don't underestimate the power of scent. A signature fragrance in your stores or packaging can do wonders. Does your brand own any signature smell?
- **Gustatory**: Enhancing taste or flavor profiles can be a game-changer in food, beverage, or cosmetics.
- **Tactile**: Materials matter. From packaging texture to product ergonomics, what people touch shapes their emotional feelings.

But don't try to do everything at once. Prioritize based on:
- Brand relevance—does this change align with our identity?
- Emotional resonance—will it stir the right feelings?
- Feasibility—how easy (or hard) is it to implement?

The Outcome: A Sensory Strategy That Goes Beyond Words

Once you're done, you'll have something precious—clarity.
- Clarity on the sensory memories you already own in the hearts and minds of consumers.
- Insight into subconscious brand equity—the stuff you can't see on a balance sheet.
- And most importantly, a roadmap to build emotional differentiation through intentional sensory design.

This isn't a one-time thing either. You can revisit the framework every year, or before significant moments such as a rebrand, a new product launch, or a retail makeover.

Think of this framework not just as an audit but as a ritual—a way to ensure your brand continues to live not just in ads or social media but in people's memories, bodies, and emotions.

At the end of the day, people don't just buy products—they buy based on how those products make them *feel*. And Sensory Memories play a big part in defining this.

30

PUTTING THEORY INTO PRACTICE: SENSORY MEMORY IN ACTION

We've talked about how each of the 6Ps – Product, Price, Place, Promotion, People, and Process – can trigger sensory memories that stick with consumers long after the moment has passed. But what does that actually look like in the real world?

Let's bring this idea to life by examining two brands that almost everyone knows and loves: **Starbucks** and **Oreo**. These brands have built incredibly strong emotional and sensory associations over the years. Think about it: the sound of your name being called out at Starbucks, or the satisfying crunch of an Oreo dipped in milk. These aren't just experiences – they're memories your senses hold onto.

Below, we've mapped out how each of these iconic brands activates the five key sensory memories – **Visual, Sonic, Olfactory, Gustatory, and Tactile** – across each of the **6Ps** of marketing. It's like a sensory x-ray of brand magic in action. Ready to explore? Let's dive in.

A. Starbucks: Sensory Memory Illustration

Let's start with the **Starbucks** example — a globally recognized brand with rich multi-sensory branding. Here's how **Starbucks** engages the **five sensory memories** (Visual, Sonic, Olfactory, Gustatory, Tactile) across the **6Ps of marketing**:

PRODUCT (The actual coffee, food, packaging)

Sensory Type	Brand Memory (Starbucks)
Visual	Green mermaid logo, cup size naming (Tall, Grande, Venti), latte art, clean modern typography
Sonic	Espresso machine steam, café ambient jazz, customer name being called out
Olfactory	Signature roasted coffee aroma when you enter
Gustatory	The distinct bittersweet taste of the espresso blend, seasonal drinks like the Pumpkin Spice Latte
Tactile	The warm cup sleeve texture, the premium feel of the cup, and the bakery packaging

PRICE (How price is communicated and perceived)

Sensory Type	Brand Memory (Starbucks)
Visual	Price boards with elegant font, app-based pricing interface
Sonic	Subtle 'cha-ching' of digital transactions, mobile payment "beep" sound
Olfactory	Not directly relevant, but could associate the smell of premium = justifies price
Gustatory	Perception that "this taste is worth the price" – crafted flavor = premium value
Tactile	Premium card texture (Starbucks card), thick takeaway napkins

SENSORY BRAND AUDIT

PLACE (Café interiors, layout, accessibility)

Sensory Type	Brand Memory (Starbucks)
Visual	Earth-toned wood decor, soft lighting, and global consistency in design
Sonic	Chill music playlists curated to mood, soft coffee shop buzz
Olfactory	Consistent coffee bean smell across all outlets globally
Gustatory	Free water or testers, store-exclusive flavor options
Tactile	Plush sofas, solid wooden tables, textured wall finishes

PROMOTION (Advertising, app notifications, digital presence)

Sensory Type	Brand Memory (Starbucks)
Visual	Green-themed seasonal campaigns, Instagramable cup photos
Sonic	Audio branding in ads, holiday jingle "sip the season"
Olfactory	Scratch-and-sniff ads (in rare campaigns) for new flavors
Gustatory	Limited-time flavor trials or samplings during campaigns
Tactile	Special edition cup textures, gift cards with embossing

PEOPLE (Baristas, customer interaction, service tone)

Sensory Type	Brand Memory (Starbucks)
Visual	Barista uniforms, name tags, and friendly smiles
Sonic	Personalized greetings, "Kashika, your drink is ready!", in happy tones
Olfactory	Perfume-free staff ensures the coffee scent is dominant
Gustatory	Barista-made custom drinks remembered over time
Tactile	Friendly handshake or handing over the drink with a warm sleeve

PROCESS (Ordering, delivery, app UX)

Sensory Type	Brand Memory (Starbucks)
Visual	Clean app interface, progress bar visuals while waiting
Sonic	Notification tone when your order is ready, app sound effects
Olfactory	Drive-through window still releasing coffee scent
Gustatory	Consistency of taste regardless of outlet or country
Tactile	Tapping on the app, gripping the drink holder tray, and the loyalty card

B. OREO: Sensory Memory Illustration

Now let's take a popular **packaged consumer good** – for example, **Oreo (by Mondelez)** – and map out **sensory memories** across the **6Ps** using the **five sensory types**:

PRODUCT (The Oreo biscuit itself, its variants, and packaging)

Sensory Type	Brand Memory (Oreo)
Visual	Distinct black-and-white cookie, blue packaging, milk splash graphics
Sonic	Iconic "twist, lick, dunk" sound ritual; crunch of the biscuit
Olfactory	Sweet chocolatey-vanilla smell when the pack is opened
Gustatory	Familiar sweet cocoa biscuit + creamy filling taste; distinct even in blind tests
Tactile	Crumbly outer biscuit, smooth inner cream; ridged pack texture

PRICE (How the price is presented, perceived value)

Sensory Type	Brand Memory (Oreo)
Visual	Price tags on shelf, value packs, multipack design
Sonic	Supermarket announcements: "Buy 1 Get 1 Oreo today!"
Olfactory	N/A, but sometimes association of premium = intense chocolate aroma
Gustatory	"Tastes like more than what it costs" – high reward at a low price point
Tactile	Larger packs = bulk feel = more value in hand

PLACE (Retail shelf, visibility, availability)

Sensory Type	Brand Memory Oreo)
Visual	Easy-to-spot blue packets on the shelf, stack displays, shelf trays
Sonic	Crinkling plastic when a shopper picks up or opens a pack
Olfactory	Not often relevant in retail, but smell is sometimes present in open grocery areas
Gustatory	Often given in sampling events, kids' fairs, etc.
Tactile	Shelf-ready packs, hanging packs for modern trade, bulkier family packs for supermarkets

PROMOTION (Advertising, online campaigns, influencers)

Sensory Type	Brand Memory (Oreo)
Visual	Playful black-and-white ads, kids dunking cookies, and blue-white campaign visuals
Sonic	TV/radio jingle "Twist, Lick, Dunk!" or crunch sound in ads
Olfactory	Not common, but experiential campaigns could include scent in pop-ups
Gustatory	Tasting booths in malls, promo samples of new flavors
Tactile	Limited-edition embossed packaging, influencer unboxings with unique textures

PEOPLE (Brand reps, in-store promoters, emotional bonding)

Sensory Type	Brand Memory (Oreo)
Visual	In-store promoters in Oreo-themed uniforms
Sonic	Promoters saying, "Try the new Oreo Red Velvet!" or mom's voice saying, "Have an Oreo."
Olfactory	Subtle cookie scent used in some pop-up campaigns
Gustatory	Emotional association of mom giving Oreo to child, school tiffin box memory
Tactile	Hands-on moment of dipping the Oreo in milk – sensory ritual

PROCESS (How it's bought, opened, consumed)

Sensory Type	Brand Memory (Oreo)
Visual	Easy-tear "open tab" on pack, resealable designs, pouch shapes
Sonic	Sound of plastic rip and cookie crunch – highly distinctive
Olfactory	Instant sweet, chocolatey aroma when the pack is opened
Gustatory	Step-by-step taste ritual: twist, lick, dunk, bite
Tactile	Hard biscuit, soft cream, cold milk combo – multisensory ritual

Now It's Your Turn: Does Your Brand Own a Sensory Memory?

So now that you've seen how brands like **Starbucks** and **Oreo** effortlessly weave themselves into our sensory memories... here's the big question: **What about your brand?**

Close your eyes for a second and ask yourself –

- When someone sees your product, do they instantly recognize it?
- Can they hear your brand before they even see it
- Do they associate a certain smell, taste, or touch with you, something only you own?

If you answered **yes** to most of these, congratulations – your brand is probably killing it in the market. You've built more than awareness; you've built **memory**. But if you're still unsure, or if there are a few blanks in your sensory map, then hey, you've just found your next challenge.

The good news? You've got the framework. You've got the tools. Now, it's time to craft experiences that not only **reach your consumer**... but **stay with them.**

REFERENCES

1. Kahneman, D. (2011). *Thinking, fast and slow*. Farrar, Straus and Giroux.
2. Damasio, A. R. (1994). *Descartes' error: Emotion, reason, and the human brain*. Putnam.
3. LeDoux, J. (1996). *The emotional brain: The mysterious underpinnings of emotional life*. Simon & Schuster.
4. Ariely, D. (2008). *Predictably irrational: The hidden forces that shape our decisions*. HarperCollins.
5. Dooley, R. (2012). *Brainfluence: 100 ways to persuade and convince consumers with neuromarketing*. Wiley.
6. Plassmann, H., Ramsøy, T. Z., & Milosavljevic, M. (2012). Branding the brain: A critical review and outlook. *Journal of Consumer Psychology*, 22(1), 18–36.
7. Greenwald, A. G., McGhee, D. E., & Schwartz, J. L. (1998). Measuring individual differences in implicit cognition: The Implicit Association Test. *Journal of Personality and Social Psychology*, 74(6), 1464–1480.
8. Luck, S. J. (2014). *An introduction to the event-related potential technique* (2nd ed.). MIT Press.
9. Wedel, M., & Pieters, R. (2007). *Eye tracking for visual marketing*. Now Publishers Inc.

10. Levitin, D. J. (2006). *This is your brain on music: The science of a human obsession*. Dutton.

11. Juslin, P. N., & Västfjäll, D. (2008). Emotional responses to music. *Behavioral and Brain Sciences*, 31(5), 559–575.

12. Zatorre, R. J., & Salimpoor, V. N. (2013). Music and neural substrates. *PNAS*, 110(S2), 10430–10437.

13. Krishna, A. (2012). *Customer sense: How the 5 senses influence buying behavior*. Palgrave Macmillan.

14. Spence, C. (2021). *Sensehacking: How to use the power of your senses for happier, healthier living*. Viking.

15. Gallace, A., & Spence, C. (2014). *In touch with the future: The sense of touch from cognitive neuroscience to virtual reality*. Oxford University Press.

16. Keller, K. L. (2003). *Strategic brand management* (2nd ed.). Prentice Hall.

17. Cialdini, R. B. (2006). *Influence: The psychology of persuasion*. Harper Business.

18. Heath, C., & Heath, D. (2007). *Made to stick: Why some ideas survive and others die*. Random House.

19. Tegmark, M. (2017). *Life 3.0: Being human in the age of artificial intelligence*. Knopf.

20. Sani, O. G., et al. (2021). Mind-reading BCIs using AI. *Nature Neuroscience*, 24(4), 509–519.

ABOUT THE AUTHOR

Mahesh Agarwal is the Co-founder and Managing Director of **Neurosensum**, a pioneering neuroscience-based market research company. With a degree in **Behavioural Economics** and an **MBA**, Mahesh brings over **30 years of experience** in marketing research, blending traditional insights with cutting-edge neuroscience tools.

Starting his career in conventional research, Mahesh was always intrigued by one question: *How does the human brain really make decisions?* This curiosity led him to the emerging field of **Consumer Neuroscience**, where he found a powerful way to bridge the gap between what consumers say and what they truly feel.

Over the years, he has developed multiple **neuro-based frameworks and products** that help marketers understand their audiences at a deeper, subconscious level.

Mahesh has presented several papers at **ESOMAR**, the world's leading organization for market researchers, and continues to advocate for the integration of neuroscience into mainstream marketing. His passion for making **neuromarketing accessible and actionable** is one of the driving forces behind this book. Originally from India, Mahesh moved to **Jakarta, Indonesia**, nearly two decades ago. He has since fallen in love with the country's vibrant food, natural beauty, and warm-hearted people. On weekends, you'll often find him on road trips with his wife **Kanchana** and their close-knit circle of friends, exploring the hidden gems around Jakarta.

www.ingramcontent.com/pod-product-compliance
Lightning Source LLC
Chambersburg PA
CBHW031626160426
43196CB00006B/297